With Folded Wings

by

Stewart Edward White

"Walk through your days as a creature with folded wings, conscious of the possession of another element and your ability to enter it."

INVISIBLE

ISBN: 978-1-78139-001-6

Front cover: *Christis in the sepulchre, guarded by angels*
by William Blake

"Caterpillar on the end of a twig; and he's eaten all the leaves and got to the end of the twig; and he's crying, because all the food in the world is eaten up, and the race of caterpillars is going to die! Besides, he's pushing out into the air in every direction, and he says he's found out everything; no place else to go. It's only a little twig, too. And he thinks that if he dies there aren't going to be any more caterpillars! ... Wait a minute, the caterpillar is saying something: that he doesn't know what's going to happen to the work of the Creator. Creator isn't going to have anything more to do; He's finished; because he (the caterpillar) was the Crowning Work, and when he's gone...

"Never saw a caterpillar cry before – it's funny. Well, it's a tragedy. All the work of the Creator is coming to an end in the highest possible thing – and he's going to die! He says there'll be nobody to pass on his enormous experience to! He's going to make a mummy case, and crawl into it – no matter how the Creator feels about it. He'll do it to spite Him. He doesn't know he's going to be a butterfly. He's crying because he's sorry for himself; he really believes he's sorry for God – all His wonderful creative work going to end! That's a sad picture!"

"Well," said the Invisible, "that's the way most of your sad pictures look from this side."

"There he goes, into his mummy case. He's shutting the door and saying: 'That's that! I'll bet God'll be sorry that He fixed it so there's nowhere else for me to go – and nothing more for me to find out!' ... Bing! There's the door shut. And a little squeaky voice coming out says. – 'A-a-ll over!'

"Damfool! He doesn't know how funny he is."

"No damfool ever knows how funny he is," observed the Invisible.

"Crying because he doesn't know he's going to be a butterfly."

"No, he wouldn't want to be a butterfly," concluded the Invisible, "because he's never been one!"

ORIGINAL PUBLISHER'S NOTE

The completed manuscript of WITH FOLDED WINGS came to the Publisher from the late Stewart Edward White only a few days before his death.

As a general thing, Mr. White made a few corrections and emendations in the text of the work while it was going through the press and it is reasonable to suppose that he might have done so in the present instance, but the suddenly fatal termination of his illness rendered this impossible.

The text of WITH FOLDED WINGS here presented is, therefore, with the exception of the correction of type-errors, exactly that of the copy received from Mr. White, without either editing or revision.

Introduction

THE MATERIAL for this book is drawn from some 2,500 single-typed pages of verbatim records. The latter are made up of communications from discarnate entities we called the Invisibles, mainly through the mediumship of one of us known as Betty. The latter had become a station for this sort of transmission only by dint of a rigorous twenty years of training. This training, according to the Invisibles, was intended not so much for development in mediumship as a means toward expansion of consciousness. The resulting psychic powers were an accompaniment, a by-product. In themselves they were not the aim. The real aim, it now seems to me, was – and is – a demonstration in attainment of what Bucke named Cosmic Consciousness. But with this important advancement. The examples Bucke cites[*] experienced Cosmic Consciousness as an illumination, sudden and brief. He adds that it is probable that this state, touched only momentarily and by illumination, is the state of consciousness toward which evolution is developing.

The aim of Betty's training, and the experience she encountered in the course of it, might seem to imply that she was demonstrating a step in that evolution. She was exemplifying, in her own person, what is to be the process by which the human soul will gain permanently Cosmic Consciousness. She herself

---

[*] *Cosmic Consciousness*, by Richard M. Bucke (New York: E. P. Dutton & Co., Inc.).

entered it again and again, but only in her trance state. She reported back, and her reports have the same quality and contact that Bucke describes as the "illuminated moment" in the examples he cites. Furthermore, at the very last of her life here she won to that insight, that condition of soul, in her waking state. This laboratory demonstration of our soul's future has a profound significance.

But incidental to this, we set down the aforementioned records and communications, which dealt with Betty's training – expositions on technique, helpful comment on how to live, enunciation of principles. From them, over several years, we have compiled, generally under the further direction of the Invisibles, several books.[*] Subsequent to Betty's death, in 1939, she reversed the process, and through the mediumship of a friend whom we named Joan, she produced that amazing "divulgence," *The Unobstructed Universe.* In addition, two other books whose contents were not so directly quoted from the records nevertheless fitted in as part of the whole effort.[†]

That would seem to cover the field. But a rereading of those 2,500 pages convinced me that the present volume was also part of the pattern. The remaining material was too richly significant to ignore. Furthermore, it covered aspects of this expansion of consciousness business not dealt with in the other books.

---

[*] *The Betty Book, Across the Unknown, The Road I Know* (New York: E. P. Dutton & Co., Inc.).

[†] *Anchors to Windward, The Stars Are Still There* (New York: E. P. Dutton & Co., Inc).

Nonetheless in a very few instances the logical sequence demanded a brief repeat of a paragraph or so that had already been used. This is due warning that such is the case. So if some reader recognizes a passage here and there, he will understand that it is an intentional inclusion. This being once and for all understood, I have felt justified in omitting footnote references that would merely clutter up the page.

There remains but one further explanation. Most of this is form or through Betty, and is so labeled. A few others, which are ascribed simply to "the Station," came through two people who developed their mediumship with Betty and did nearly all of their work in either her presence or mine. We have been given to understand that the communications are an essential part of the complete picture.

Contents

I The Aim

I DON'T want to preach at anybody; I just want to share something beautiful. The true teacher brings his own iris of beauty to you without proselytizing, I, without thrusting things at you. He makes you remind YOURSELF of the deep blue sky and the fluttering gold of autumn, or the thrill of fern fronds and the sweet stirring earth of spring. A man like that who stimulates living is his own sermon.

BETTY

— 1 —

SINCE WE are not ourselves ultimates, we cannot know ultimate Purpose. The present purpose seems to be evolution by means of functioning. The objective of evolution is twofold. On the one hand it is the development of the independent individual. On the other it is the coordination of the individuals so developed into a functioning Unity.

This dual objective is the Aim with which we must be concerned. It is the rod by which we must measure our ambitions, activities and deeds. Are they in furtherance of this Universal Aim? Provincial divergences of ethics must yield to this simple criterion. So the development of ourselves as individuals in evolution becomes our first obligation.

— 2 —

When this doctrine of self-development was first

offered us by the Invisibles we shied away. In common with most of our generation we had been brought up on an ethic of "doing for others," of "unselfishness," of "service." We had not lived up to that ideal. As children we had often endured the finger of scorn and the epithet "Selfish!" And has grown-ups we had more than once had an uncomfortable feeling we were not "doing our duty" by others. The idea that maybe we had been at least partly right all along looked too much like wishful thinking.

But the Invisibles persisted. A little here, a little there, they infiltrated their subject. Finally they treated it to a full-length discourse.

"You must," said they, "learn to understand what necessary over-emphasis has obscured. This is that the word 'selfish' has also an obverse, a meaning of usefulness, even a meaning of necessity. Like all ingredients of life, it has its necessary proportion.

"Your first duty in development, not only for your own sake but for the sake of the greater whole, is the establishment of a homogeneous, close-knit, invulnerable core of yourself as an individual. Until you have so established a center or nucleus, no matter how small, in which your conviction is absolute that it is the germ center of yourself as a separate eternal entity in cosmos, any venturing outside your boundaries is unwarranted and will inevitably prove more or less disastrous. Even the natural instinctive eagerness of outfling must be withheld until that sure core of integration is assured.

"This primary central establishment is the first indispensable step in the creation of the eternal self.

Whether it takes a decade, a half-century, a whole lifetime, or the repeated incarnations of a number of phases, *no forward movement can safely, effectively or constructively be attempted until this is accomplished.* OUTSIDE engagements can succeed only after this fact. Thenceforward this central self becomes a citadel for withdrawal from mistaken or premature outgoings. Such outgoings, before the complete and homogeneous occupation of this center, leave a tenuosity behind your back permeable by usurping forces which a firmer establishment would have automatically excluded. Therefore, stop *at this point of development* until the assurance is gained, no matter what implication even to yourself such a course may seem to have of selfishness, self-centeredness, lack of outside response and responsibility, or any of the other reproachful concepts of which this use is the constructive obverse.

"Here is a truth so profound and yet so simply stated that I would have it in a separate paragraph:

"Outgivng is never constructively effective unless it is an overflow."

"You may out-give by pumping up, generally with the suction of what is expected, or the proper thing, or the duty, or the obligation to the world or humanity, general or specific. But pumping up always means depletion; depletion means vacuum; and vacuum is a vortex of attraction for the destructive. Overflow, on the other hand, is a super-abundance that leaves no lack behind it, but still the filled reservoir of accomplishment. When you rush forth to give, driven by your natural instincts of sympathy, of desire to reconstruct, of sensitivity to conditions, pause to consider whether you are leaving your territory unoccupied, open to an invasion that ultimately is going to make you ineffective. Your responsibility as a component part of the greater whole is primarily yourself, and only secondarily that which you accomplish outside yourself. That the secondary may be important is acknowledged, *but it is impossible* that it should be aught but ephemeral if the primary is not a solid reality. In this sense it is your *business* to be selfish, in the shining aspect of that word. And the great paradox is that the shining use of selfishness enables you to be effectively, and without disintegration, what the world calls 'unselfish.'"

— 3 —

As a rule the Invisibles waited for us to practice what they preached before they gave explanations. The idea seemed to be that only in this way could we accomplish anything permanent. Otherwise it would not be ourselves who accomplished. It would be merely the acceptance of someone else's accomplishment. And that is never permanent.

It was just this way in the present case. But eventually they gave us more insight into how this self-development thing worked.

"The individual man," said they, "is a member of not one narrow group only, such as the family. He is also a member of a succession of ever more inclusive groups, until he is to be considered eventually a member of that which comprises the sum total of earthly incarnations. Each of these groups has its own type of problems, good and evil, to be worked out. And all of these problems have the same characteristic of being beyond the scope and power of individual solution. They have also the characteristic in common that they are the individual problem and responsibility.

"From this it follows that if an individual works out his own development, he automatically also works out, as far as the individual can, the group problem. And consequently, if the group problem is by so much carried out, there is so much less of it to weigh upon the other members of the group. In that thought you may glimpse the interrelations of effort, and the value to others of whatever real progress you make for yourself. You may also, perhaps, glimpse the reverse, and perceive how imposing additional limitations on yourself through inertia and indifference does likewise to others. This is for the automatic relationships.

"There enters also a semi-automatic relationship, as one might say. If the individual works out within himself his own portion of the group Impetus, he will in the process, by a universal law, have produced something which manifests that bit of development in the external world. It may be a concrete thing, or a bit of practical knowledge, or merely an externalized spiritual attitude. But whatever its form, it is there existent in an appropriatable shape for those who can reach out for it and utilize it. And whenever such an appropriation is made by another, not only does the utilization aid further in the solving of that group problem, but also in repercussion it renders stable the advancement of the one first attaining."

"Then," commented one of us, "it really is legitimate to pursue personal ambitions!"

"Surely!" was the reply. "One should build one's self the best possible. The trouble often is that that becomes both sufficient and inviolable. One forgets that the building of one's self is but for the purpose of contributing one's self-contributing one's self *completely*. That may sound out of reach, impractical, even undesirable. And maybe it is – for the present. Nevertheless it is an eventuality to be faced, for the things we hold back are what keep us from participation in the greater Whole."

– 4 –

So indispensable to the longer view of evolution is this imperative of self-development that to it we may ascribe the urgency of one of mankind's deepest instincts. Like other basic instincts, at this stage of human development it is more often perverted than not. But the handicap of present perversion is a lesser price to pay for the later perfected function. I refer here to the acquisitional sense.

This instinct expresses itself in a thousand forms. It is a fruitful cause of injustice, greed, wars, all the less pretty manifestations. Yet we could not exist, much less advance in evolution, without it. It has also its higher manifestations, and they are worth waiting for and paying for. In order that our level of abundance may rise to the point of overflow.

"Like everything else," said the Invisibles, "the acquisitional sense can be transposed from the gathering together of things – often a necessary and valuable pursuit – to intangible and more valuable purposes. Also we can acquire by drawing entirely to ourselves and keeping what we gain, or we can acquire what is necessary for a *forthgoing plan*. This second form of acquisitiveness is manifested in countless ways, from the hungers of the body, which are hungers of purpose beyond the mere possession of the immediate object, to the farthest reaches of man's serving of his destiny. Viewed thus from a height, this impulse we inadequately call the acquisitive sense is but the ambition of an artist seeking finer and still finer materials for his creative purposes. Break the health of this function and you destroy man's reason for being."

Betty was introduced to this higher acquisitiveness in one of her symbolic experiences with the Invisibles.

"It is hard to tell you of this,", she said, "because I know so little about it, but it rests on firm sane laws. It is hidden under the surface glint of materially desirable things. Those who never possess these sometimes find the secret of possession of all life; and those who have satiated themselves come painfully to starvation on golden platters: and some in between acquire the balance which directs them to the secret of possession.

"I cannot grow in a moment to where I can describe this vivid contrast in the methods of ownership: ownership after the manner of man, and ownership by way of the law. I can only just sense it by looking at my associates here. Because today I am in the company of those who have completely abandoned self for the heritage of participating in the whole. They are absolutely dispossessed of things. They've grown into enormous, almost unlimited power by the strength of their aims. I don't understand it. I only know their power is a kind of selfless power which makes their position unrelated to any of the products we call possessions.

(long pause)

"I was experimentally broadcasting myself to participation in the great elements of life, and I said: Why do I not come to dissolution of my individuality this way? And then I dimly sensed the use of that other gathering-in, collecting instinct in its unperverted state. I sensed its ability to concentrate power collected to be utilized for the intelligent purposes of cooperation. But I'm too feeble and stupid to tell you much that is useful...

"Here are two great forces. I must leave them there."

II Education

I WANT just to swing on a gate and look at things go by and think how nice the world is and how something exciting might happen.

BETTY

— 1 —

SELF-DEVELOPMENT, then, is our first aim in life. I place it first, in time if not in importance, because no coordination of individuals is possible until said individuals are first established. Another priority: before we can do a thing well we have to learn how. And learning how is education.

So it will be profitable to examine what the Invisibles had to say to us, at different times, on this subject. On this subject in general, I hasten to add; for the particular details of our own individual training have been elsewhere set down. What broad principles could the Invisibles suggest to us?

"We will not consider education in any narrow or restricted sense of the word," they once told us. "We endeavor to tell you of the process by which personality comes into being out of the totality of existence; how it gains self-consciousness and vision of its purpose which is its only excuse for being. The cosmic task is to gain self-knowledge and self-control. Individually we need go no further than that our task also is to acquire self-knowledge and self-control, in order that through the exercise of free will we may assemble conditions for the satisfaction of our creative instinct.

"Education, then, in the largest sense, is the assembling of such conditions as will facilitate making habits of right choice, actuated by the creative instinct, and inspired by the disciplined imagination which senses the glory of the Pattern.

"Therefore, the teacher – which includes parents of both sexes – is under obligation to assemble those conditions in which the self-preservative instincts – to state it in its lowest terms – shall find it advantageous to acquire habits that will be of the most practical use to the individual as such, and at the same time the most socially effective.

"Or perhaps," they continued laying this cosmic foundation, "we might define education as the process of gradually changing the emphasis of the underlying instincts from the egocentric to the altruistic.

"And remember," they concluded, "that the little child is the type; both of the task and of those who must perform it. For you and we, viewed from the eminence of that Cosmic Purpose, are only little children feeling our way."

– **2** –

In the light of that statement, the methods of parent-teacher with children become of vital significance in hinting a clue for the most effective way to go about our own adult self-education. The best insight we were given into the child's own reactions came from one of Betty's symbolic experiences in which she seemed actually to become the person she described. In this case a small boy enduring too common grown-up ideas of training.

"How absurd!" she began. "What a ridiculous game! I don't reduce very well, do I? I can't stay long enough in it – like a rubber band springing back.

"I am in a tall and incorrigibly rigid world. There are many fascinating things; but they are all guarded by dragons of fierce and painful penalties. How stupid to make so amusing a world so difficult! It is a child's near-sighted world; and all these horrid grown-ups have such far-sighted penalties!

(laughs)

"I'm so amused at myself: this Lilliputian game is so absurd!

"The world could be quite nice; but it's like a nightmare of scene-shifters, always thrusting forward obstructions to shut out the wide world. One could make one's way along very comfortably, taking things as they come, if it weren't for those obstructions that they are always running across one's path. It stiffens and spoils everything, makes a cross feeling.

"Don't you see? That sort of thing immediately makes you fighting obstinate to see the other side, to get beyond the obstruction. It is maddening to be always thwarted that way, just as you get started. That's what makes him so wild later, this constant confusing and thwarting of contrary purposes around him. This is the chief warping of him. That makes the obstinate streak, the dogged, blind, pig-headedness being bred in him. That's the flaw: going right along increasing.

"He's a nice, cheerful, likeable boy, when you don't touch this particular sore spot. Nice boy; not too thick-skinned, but certainly not very sensitive; capable of average modeling – perhaps a little above the average."

(pause)

"Terribly oppressive, the contact with grown-ups, isn't it? So deadening. They have no understanding of what you are talking about. And they tell you stuff you can't grasp and that just puzzles you. Pretty soon you shut down and don't try.

"He wishes he could be a newsboy, like the one who comes with the paper. Such a devilish kind of a person! He hurls in the paper all folded up tight; and lops away on his bicycle, first on one side and then on the other, and he generally tries to be funny. Anyway, he has a great life!

"What a nuisance thinking is, isn't it? It is so much pleasanter just rhythmically to repeat gestures or words without having to tic them down to anything. It is the pinning-down-of-things that grown-ups do that's so hard. It is so much pleasanter not to THINK. You just start the hammock going and get the swing of it...

(pause)

"See? The child is coming out of that rhythm, and the fixation of things is a tremendous struggle. We forget how much of a struggle it is... See how the rhythm is slowing down? It's slowing down; it's getting fixed. It's like putting pins in some fluttering wings... No: it's a natural development; it's not painful, like pinning wings. It's a natural process. It slows down naturally. That transition is what makes contact with the experiences of life. It should be carefully handled. Jars are what do the damage, the clumsy handling of well-meaning grown-ups. It is very important that it should be done, though.

"Isn't it curious, the proportion of life that is spent in directing the plastic little mind toward the proprieties and what is spent toward the principles of living? The proprieties are all right, but they are not nine-tenths. They are only the door-men for the principles."

— 3 —

Next day Betty continued with her symbolic experience. Once more she explored the point of view of the harassed small boy.

"You've seen a bumble-fly go around the ceiling," she said, "bumping and bumping in circles, trying to find a way out. It's like that, the way a child is always restlessly picking and breaking, trying to find its way out. You cannot understand how the bulk of your assimilated experience looks to a child who has not digested it. And we give so niggardly of it! 'What's that thing for?' 'Oh, that? That's just a ding-bat.'

"All you know of its history and use denied to the child. He has no contact of interest with it. Everything is kept away up in grown-up G.

"Even the well-meaning grown-ups will not reduce their material. They insist on giving it whole, instead of in assimilable little bits patiently administered. How stupid we are; and how contented *they* are in many ways. It's lucky they are, or we'd all mold them on our mistakes...

(pause)

"There's that poor sullen boy again. He's not sullen as much as thwarted some way, undeveloped. Poor little stiffening mind! They are working so much with that organ they're stiffening it, and it is exceedingly uncomfortable. It is something like a valve that normally should be open, but by too-constant pressure, more than it can stand, it acquires a spastic way of closing. A fatal habit! It is not his strongest faculty anyway, mental effort; and by hectoring they've spoiled the natural resiliency of that open valve. They've caused this nervous hysterical action of closing instantly when approached; a kind of self-protection against too great strain. The boy didn't have the caliber for it.

"Now I will stay still and see if I can get the contrasting opposite. That little valve would have stayed open if it had been left alone until it had matured. Seems not to have been particularly backward; but too early, too vigorously, too unwisely tampered with. Should have had little bits of food daily. It is a most precious thing, his keeping open that valve in the mind, that desire for knowledge, that ability to listen, that confidence in approaching subjects, instead of a shutdown antagonistic attitude...

"It is very difficult for me to keep down here, to keep to this level. I begin to get interested, and at once I over-age myself in my point of view. I have got to stay down here as well as I can without trying any grown-up interpretations..."

(pause)

"Well it's springtime; very exciting. My, the outside-the-windows feels nice when you lean out! How much nicer the world is outside the windows than in! More understandable. Everything is so soft and velvety; kind of warm-damp feeling. For some reason it's a particularly exciting day... Only he doesn't think about it; just feels."

At this point an Invisible took over to interpolate: "This response of the human plant to growing impulses would be the same in his 'indoor' environment, if it were properly adjusted to his expansion. The trouble is we always try to drag children out of their simple little childhood gardens into our formal landscaped ones. They *should* absorb their experience of living naturally and eagerly. Therefore the open pores of the mind – what she calls a valve – should be the first consideration. In some children it is dominant enough to stand rough handling; with others it takes more restraint and care to develop more slowly, fed by mere bits of natural proclivities. This particular boy should have had more freedom of mind, should have been let alone in the spaces of childhood. They crowded his childhood spaces."

"As near as I can see it," said Betty, "the only practical method is bit-by-bit acquisition – even for us grown-ups. What a blessed thing it is that the Great Plan is concealed from us. We couldn't stand it. That's what's the matter with the child: they thrust the grown-up plan on him, instead of keeping him in ignorance of it and letting him take it bit by bit in daily doses. It's the way they have taught us, our Invisibles."

This is a most significant statement. After a moment she resumed the narrative of her experience.

"Now I've got to be that newsboy for a while...

"He has a moderate neglect that is very satisfactory from his point of view. He is flopping along through the spring morning, keenly open-pored, and very puppy-energied. He is in good condition for most any experience that comes along, but there is no one to direct his growth, no helping hand to point the way to education. He hasn't been damaged, but neither has he been cultivated. He's just a nice brave weed."

"The triumph of civilization is when the undamaged plant is assisted naturally to acquire the experiences which develop," the Invisible took it up. "These two boys should be utilized as foils; neither extolling the virtuous poor, nor condemning the strictures of the rich; but visualizing natural growth regardless of material circumstances as the all-important.

"If parents could hold that ideal, how rapidly the race would move. These little plant-minds in the garden of childhood are as precious and as easily damaged as windflowers, yet see how steadily they grow in natural conditions. The successful educator must enter that garden of childhood, if his wisdom will let him. Sometimes that wisdom gets so bulky that he can't get through until he obtains a finer kind. Then he can present his wisdom, quite humbly, and see what the child picks out. That's the only way to begin. Only the child knows what he can see. The educator continues offering it, supplying it, but not forcing it."

"There is so much of this child's stuff," said Betty, "but I think I can get enough of it in one more time."

— 4 —

Some days later Betty concluded childhood experience.

"I don't know what's happening," she began. "I can't think and I can't talk. Curious state!"

Ensued a long pause, necessary, it would seem, to reenter her former state.

"Now I'm in the child's world again... Funny little unthinking automatic animal: I'm reduced to that state now...

"I am lying on my back and kicking at that dangling rope, over and over and over again, first with one foot, then with the other, without variation, perfectly content. There is the feel of the sun and the breeze. Vacancy of mind.

" I, in trying to make out why this thing is so important, why this state of fallowness is so important to the child's growth. It is what keeps him from closing up, tightening up. A rest period, strengthening his developing faculties. He needs so much of it: it's like feeding him.

My, what nice relaxation and replenishment! Every hour of the day, nearly, is planned for. He doesn't often get this kind of a chance to straighten out. Nature just grabs it, clutches it in dire need. There's not a thought in his poor little slow brain, except a delicious numbness. You wouldn't think lying on your back and kicking at a dangling rope with your feet could be so *altogether* satisfactory!

"My, but the sun feels good! Guess I'll roll over on my stomach and feel how warm these boards are. Wow! That sensation of warmth and happiness is all through me.

" Mother Nature has reclaimed her baby. She is teaching quietly and silently the part of him that is being left uneducated. The little shy spirit is creeping out to investigate the universe outside its body-prison. Poor little house mate, it has to live like a slave below the level of the daily consciousness. Now it has come timidly out and is reviving itself. It is growing in companionship of other things of the spirit. That valve is open. Happiness, comfort, confidence are reestablished by the magic adjustors. If left unstrained and uncontracted now, the energy acquisition of life experience would assert itself: the boy would be whole and normal again.

"I'm so puzzled at these day dreams; how they

are converted into energy, and how they go wrong when you dream too much...

"There are some very wise and tender grown-ups, and they are tiptoeing into this child-land world. Why, you can come in and out, and bring almost anything in, if you do it carefully. They are not pussy-footing around either; they are just handling things with firm but tender and flexible touch. It is very nice to walk in that land when you can adjust yourself to it and do it helpfully...

"Now I am to understand that the only successful modelers of childhood are the ones who can enter this plastic state of mind, and see the strange persistent determination of young growth. It has a wise will; it knows valiantly which way it ought to go, before this directing sense is atrophied. Restriction and perversion come through too harsh handling, too much cramping into a narrow mold...

(pause)

"That was a very nice excursion! I liked that. I feel as though I had been in fairyland. You see, that explains things to me. I knew you couldn't just *abandon* a child to Mother Nature. But now I see how you should adapt knowledge to childhood. It is almost reducing it to a fluid of easily absorbed knowledge. We don't work over our kind of knowledge to digest it fur them. We try to ram it down them in the form we eat it. They take it readily enough if you prepare it.

"I can see very clearly now that rebellion of childhood. It's a kind of self-preservation."

— 5 —

This was an inside view, so to speak. On another occasion we were given the same sort of thing, but in reverse. The Station is now observing from the outside. The technique is a back and forth dialogue with an Invisible.

"He's working on a kind of picture-puzzle,"[*] reported the Station, "all sorts of queer-shaped pieces. He's just playing with the picture-puzzle. You'd better keep an eye on him, or he'll get hold of some of these ding-bats and bust something and hurt himself."

"Well, he might," conceded the Invisible, "but that's the way he's got to learn-playing with things that might hurt him. We've got to watch and see that he doesn't hurt himself, and yet learns."

"Doesn't seem to me quite fair to have this big gang of rubber-necks just watching a little kid play."

"That's the trouble with them: they never saw a child play before. He doesn't know he's playing; he's doing business, very important business. He doesn't even know he's learning; he's just got to put these together. He doesn't care whether it's important or not; it's just what he wants to do. He doesn't know there's anything else in the world except putting these together. He doesn't see you, nor the place, nor the people; he's just putting it together."

---

[*] This is one of the examples of communication independent of Betty described in the Introduction.

"Don't you see that won't fit? Let me show you."

"Get away from him: let him alone."

"But it's just a little thing to show him." Let him alone."

"But he's going to waste a lot of time trying to get that big thing in a little hole. It delays the picture."

"Let him alone."

"Now that woman over there: she's most crazy. She's got to show him.

"That's all right. If she moves, I'm going to make her sit down again. The rule is: let 'em alone. That's all the rule there is in this game."

(pause)

"Anyway, he's found that out. Looks as if he knew that. Can't make a square thing fit a round hole."

"Well, wasn't that worth finding out?"

"Why didn't he know that?"

"Well, we never get used to seeing you fellows try to fit square things in round holes."

"Look at him grin! He lit up the whole place with that smile. He found out that a round hole has to have a round thing."

"Yes, and if he was writing a book he'd probably say he'd discovered a new law of nature. (scornfully) New law! Why, that was a law before there was any Adam! That's the way man does. He stumbles over something that was always so, and he thinks he invented it."

"Say! Say kid, don't you see you've got to have a little thin thing in there? It almost fits, but it's got to have a little thin thing."

"Let him alone: don't crab the game. How is he going to learn, if you keep telling him?"

"He'll believe me."

"What of it? What if he does? If he does it because you tell him, you'll be doing it. If he finds out for himself, he will be able to do it when you are not watching. Let him alone. It's the motto of this game."

"But supposing one of those sharp things should stick into him and cut him?"

"It would only cut him once or twice. Then he'd learn that sharp things stick into him, wouldn't he? Well! What is more important: that he shouldn't cut himself, or that he should learn that sharp things stick into him? Are you going to hang around him as long as he lives, and holler to him every time a sharp thing comes along?"

(pause)

"That woman's going to have a fit!"

"Well, let her have a fit. It is more desirable that she should have a fit than that she should interfere with that child. Let 'em alone!"

"What makes him look so puzzled?"

"To save time I'll tell you. He is just beginning to get a little faint notion about the picture. He is just beginning to realize that he is doing something besides amusing himself or merely putting queer-shaped things together. There is something else going on that he does not know about. It is just beginning to dawn on him a little that if he puts them together right, something is going to happen that he did not suspect. He is just beginning to realize an intention that is bigger than his own."

"I suppose you're going to tell me that's the beginning of religion."

"Well, that's the first glimmer of human intelligence you've exhibited. You see, you're putting together a picture-puzzle too. And you can't get the picture unless every piece is in its place."

"I see. Then that wiggly one over there, that is so proudly wiggly, is holding out on the picture."

"Sure. And if you'll watch you'll see that he's got to have other wiggly ones joined up with him in a square, and he doesn't like squares. He isn't interested in the picture – not yet. He's only interested in being the only wiggly one like that."

(pause)

"Now, perhaps, you see why chlorine and sodium are put together, with all their diversity of shape and function – different kinds of wiggly ones put together right. It makes a different shaped kind of wiggly one, or maybe a square one, but it all fits in the picture."

"I can't make out whether this is an experiment in chemistry or philosophy or physics or carpentry or art or education or psychology or religion."

"Neither does anyone else; because they're all the same thing, and each one is all the others."

"That's what I call a very disorderly method of education. First thing you know, you won't be able to tell whether a fellow's an artist, or a chemist, or a preacher."

"It doesn't make any difference, does it, as long as the little fellow learns about placing the round things in the round places, and the wiggly things in the wiggly places? He is making a picture."

"Then the picture is the great thing?"

"You might say so; but I prefer to say that the little fellow is the great thing. The important thing that is going on is going on inside him. Don't you see, every time you interfere with him, you are interfering with *both* things."

"Well, can't I help him at all?"

"Sure! Give him every possible chance to learn that round things go in round holes, and that sharp things will cut, and so on. He will see the picture of his own accord as soon as it is a picture, if you give him a chance to learn how to see things by giving him things to see. If he didn't have things to see, his eyes would go dead on him. Give him practice in seeing things – but let him alone!"

Apparently this finished that aspect. But the Invisibles were not quite satisfied. Days later they suddenly returned to the dialogue as though it had never been broken off.

"She had to do that, didn't she? I thought you were going to keep her out of it," began the Station.

"I am letting her do it so you can see something."

"Agh! She thought she had to get that picture finished. She's so much smarter than he is – she thinks!"

(pause)

"He doesn't seem to be much interested in what she's doing. She keeps yanking him back to look at her doing it. He was absorbed in it until she butted in... What's she doing that for? Why doesn't she mind her own business?"

"Don't you see; she's a school ma'am and she has two reasons. She doesn't know what her reasons are; she thinks she's educating the child – that's what she says to herself. Her real reason is that she wants him to take that finished picture home and tell his mother and father that he did it, and then they'll be pleased because they'll think he is a very smart child. But she won't care so much what they think about that, as that they will think she's a very smart teacher. She's thinking not so much of the child as of herself and her job. If she were thinking about the child she would see that she is only teaching the child to lie to his father and mother in pretending that he is something he is not.

"Oh yes, he's smart enough; only she is robbing the child of his chance to acquire experience and memory, which is the indispensable attribute of personality. She kids herself with the idea that she is teaching the child. She isn't; she is robbing him for her own benefit. The joke is that by just so much as she is cheating him, she is also robbing herself. I told you that, you remember, we are not allowed to 'help' anybody when it means robbing him of his opportunity to acquire personality. It is a Law.

"You see, that kid doesn't give a hoot for what she's doing. She thinks he's there sitting beside her, because she's big enough to keep him there physically. As a matter of fact he went away some time ago and is out in the garden looking at the birds. But she doesn't know it.

"It's a very big principle. If you once get it into your head that the laws of nature operate only under the direction of Intelligence – ALL the laws – then the making of intelligence is the big thing. And the only way to acquire intelligence is through experience and the memory of it. It is possible to assimilate the experience of other people, but it is real assimilation only when you contribute an actuality of your own."

– 6 –

The last statement resulted in a side excursion into the question of the vicarious and its value or lack of value.

"Consider novels, movies, all that sort of thing," said the Invisible. "In a measure, if the novels are real and skillfully done, and the movies are wisely conceived, something does get across that is genuine experience in a way. But the majority are cheating themselves by a make-believe process. They are getting their experience cheap, just by looking at an imitation of it! They wish they could be brave and loyal and so on, so they go and look at somebody being brave and loyal, or they read about it in a book, and they get a kind of little tinkle of it – but it doesn't *cost* them anything. Or they go see things done in the way of experience or gratification that they haven't the guts to do. The potential thief gets all the temporary mistaken zest of stealing vicariously without having to go to Jail. The picture goes to jail. And don't you see, by just so much as a picture or novel deals with primitive debased instincts and gratifications, it piles up the effects of low and mean experiences and memory, and builds up a personality on the wrong side; because a man is in a very big sense the sum total of his experience and memory. And if he confines himself to low and mean experience and memory – his own or another's – he can't help being low and mean.

"There's another side to it too. When he thrills himself with second hand bravery or other fine qualities, it takes an increasing dose always to get the thrill again – when he doesn't do it himself – and after a while it doesn't act on him any more: he has to get something stronger and ranker. Then two things happen: he doesn't react to the fine things, and he has to get rawer and ranker and more debased things to tickle his palate. So he gets what the preachers call gospel-hardened – it doesn't ring his bell any more.

"I don't mean to knock novels and movies and such in any indiscriminate way. Exhibits of constructive forces in operation are good – provided they inspire to self-activity. Bravery and loyalty and all that sort of thing are no good to you as long as you just look at them: you've got to *be* them.

"On the other hand, it's easier to slide down than to climb up. Construction takes work. That's the reason why habitually looking at destructive and debasing things does you more harm than habitually merely looking at examples of constructive things does you good.

"So you must surround this little kid, not with things that will emphasize his disintegrating tendencies, but with things that will inspire he best that is in him. Don't you see what a terrific responsibility this lays

28

upon everyone who can control environment, however slightly? Never forget that you yourself, in your interplay between your own soul and its physical manifestation, are part of the environment that you are creating for that kid. Anybody who makes anything, or writes or paints or sings or behaves – anything – is making an environment for the kids, for the souls coming along; for the little hands reaching up.

"So the fellow who writes has a big job, not only to depict brave things and loyal people – for the drug-fiends of emotion to amuse themselves with, and to distract them from their own business; but to raise hell with his readers so that they will have to do it. The fellow who does his art so that it will actually *inspire up* and *retard down* is some artist!

$$-7-$$

At this point they swung back to the original discussion.

"Now that little child isn't getting anything out of the teacher's work because he isn't doing it himself. The business of education is to bring out what a child has inside; and the only way it can come out, generally speaking, is by taking the outside pressure off so it can come out. Then it win come out along the line of least resistance. But if you clamp him in, it not only does not come out, but it either goes dead on him or raises some kind of hell inside. First thing you know that kid is going to bust, and likely they'll can it mischief and spank him as a bad boy. They may even get him to thinking he is a bad boy, and he is likely to do what he thinks is expected of him. I think you quite realize that the energy that is used in badness – as it is called – is precisely the same energy that is used by the same fellow in what you call goodness. Keep your pipe loaded with that: there's only one kind of energy.

"Now education consists in supervising with the least possible interference the process of trial and error. The wise teacher helps – yes, he tells things; he gives little facts; he knows how to give little ready-made lumps of racial experience and the things he has found out himself. But he does it in such a way that it isn't a substitute for the child's own experience. His relations with the child are such that he can smuggle in sometimes a pretty good sized gob of ready-made stuff, but there's got to be a large measure of sympathy.

"Look at that word a minute. We all have enough Greek to see what it is made out of. First, *syn* – together. Second, *pathos* – feeling. Well, don't you see, the ready-made stuff doesn't get across without the *syn-pathos* – together feeling.

"There's mathematics. Mathematics is a tool, and a good one. But children get scared of it because the teacher thinks she should put on a sour face when she says mathematics, instead of smiling about it. You can teach a child anything with a smile – *syn-pathos*.

"But no amount of *syn-pathos* can take the place of experience and memory – the little kid's experience and memory. He's got to learn to use his equipment: he's got to learn to open and see through those five doors of the senses *himself*. The only way he can learn is by reaching up to the handle and trying the knob and seeing how the hinges work and making his little fat legs reach up to the step on one side and down the step on the other. You can put a little stool under his feet so he can reach, and you can have your hand ready to keep him from stumbling when he might break his neck. But it is a lot more important for experience and memory that he should learn to balance himself than that he should keep from bumping himself.

"There's a good saying that the parents – yes, and teachers (by which I mean everybody who has anything to do with him) – need only give the child tools and show him how to use them. But even that isn't true, really. He's *got* the tools, and you don't exactly show him how to use them. The only thing you can do, when you come down to brass tacks, is to give him opportunity where he can't be happy unless he uses them all. Amy kind of purpose or project that *interests* him offers opportunity for using all of them. See that he uses all of them. Don't let him get so occupied with seeing that he doesn't give a square deal to hearing, and smelling, and tasting and touching.

"You understand that the use of these tools isn't for his own sake alone. It is in order that impressions and experiences sorted out and remembered, both consciously and unconsciously, shall not only build up a body of experience and memory – which together make personality – but that that totality, that increasingly efficient totality, shall become self-conscious, self-directing, self-controlled intelligence, with the power and the right to assemble conditions for the purposes of creation."

— **8** —

"It looks," said the Invisible, "as though we had left out parental authority.

31

"You have been shown as in a vision a little child about the business of self-education, self-mastery, absorbed in a task the meaning of which he only dimly sensed, and perhaps sensed not at all. You have been adjured not to interfere unintelligently with the process. Now a narrowed view of this situation might lead you to suppose that it would be sufficient and desirable to leave the child to his own devices. Well, if I were compelled to choose between too much freedom and too much interference and superimposed authority, I think there is no doubt that too much freedom is the preferable alternative. But we are not driven to any such extreme. True, the task of education is not to drive or compel or circumscribe. But you too – as the teacher – have the duty and the privilege of exercising free will and right choice, of assembling conditions appropriate for individual development. It is for you to help make the channels through which, in the person of this developing intelligence, the power resident therein shall be directed to the fulfillment of the Pattern.

"Parental authority is a real and valuable thing, and just because it has been abused and overextended is no reason why it should be discarded entirely.

"You must remember the child is an immature thing in every way. You would not allow him to strain or injure himself by exceeding his physical powers; you would restrain him from jumping off the porch, or lifting too heavy a weight, or eating green apples or too much ice cream or cake. In doing so you are definitely exerting arbitrary parental authority in a sane, sensible and needed manner. Since the same laws work in all substances, similarly you would expect to find – and you will find – the same principle in the mental and spiritual aspects as well. There needs only wise definition of the extent and the kind of application of authority.

"All this let-him-alone advice is literally good and true. The offering of complete opportunity for self-education is the basis of all teaching. Restriction or prohibition is legitimate only when, as in the physical phase, the child is attempting to go so far beyond his powers as to injure himself or others. That does not mean he is to be inhibited when by the mere experience of defeat or disappointment he has an opportunity of extending his self-knowledge.

"In final analysis, therefore, the imposition of parental authority must depend on the wisdom of the parent. That wisdom must consist of a careful analysis, by both intellect and heart, of whether the prohibition is for the sole and only purpose of preventing an effort of one sort or another beyond the child's present strength. Just as no parent would allow the child to attempt to lift a weight beyond its muscular power, so he should not permit the child to exercise its judgment beyond its mental or spiritual power.

"I cannot point out how this is specifically to be done, for that of course depends on the individual case, and is in itself a measure of the parent's wisdom and capacity. But I do wish to call attention to the exact parallel with the merely physical training. Also I feel that some counterbalancing consideration should be introduced to prevent superficial reductio ad absurdum [literal-minded] brains from conceiving that, because we advise against herding the child too closely, we therefore advise that he should run wild."

— 9 —

Much later, after we ourselves as "children of eternity" had been at least exposed to education as the Invisibles see it, they made the adult application more directly. Their method probably is too delicate and personal for us to make more than a small beginning at its use. It is, perhaps, more in the nature of an Ultimate. Nevertheless it points a way – one that we could do well to study.

"Run your mind back," said they, "over the method employed in giving you these teachings. What was it? It was a motif with a refrain; it was a number of concepts repeated in alternation. The teachings were presented first with an experience, a parable, a symbol which entered your mind in a rather novel way, perhaps through the window instead of the front door, bringing a certain amused interest, a glimpse of something that seemed worth your intellectual attention for the moment. It escaped you very quickly, but the crack was there, the informal entrance had been made, the preparation for the second return to the subject. Next time you were a little bit more ready to receive it, more intellectually indulgent. Something obvious, perhaps, had been said, but it might possibly have value because of a telling phrase or fresh way of statement. You listened, in other words, with feeling, receptivity of heart. Germination had begun; accretions followed. The concept grew to a respectable status, worthy of your lordly mental condescension."

III Functioning

PROGRESS is the pursuit of things for which we pay the price of ourselves.

BETTY

— 1 —

AS WE have seen, in the personal case the aim is self-development. This is essentially an individual process. Therefore, it cannot be blueprinted. Nobody can give exact directions, as for the care and use of a washing machine. That is the mistake made by many systems of teaching and of religion.

"Individuality," said the Invisible, "is the end of evolution. And the higher the evolution, the more individual becomes the entity. Therefore the more individual must become its treatment."

However, it is quite possible to examine the general procedure intelligently and supply conditions that will encourage growth. We do that with plants. We have determined pretty well what happens chemically and biologically; and we supply proper soil, fertilizer, climate, water. So likewise we have a certain knowledge of the method by which we expand in consciousness. We are beginning to learn what we can supply to accelerate and foster that expansion.

— 2 —

The basic ingredients of evolution, even away down the scale, said the Invisibles, are experience and memory.

"Memory," they defined, "is a faculty which gathers or acquires certain phases from the All for the building up of that which possesses the memory. It is by the utilized memory of experience that the body of any segregated thing is expanded."

The important word here is "utilized." How do we utilize the memory of experience?

"The body of memory," said the Invisible, "acquired through the automatic awareness-responses of any entity builds up the content, not of the particular entity, but of the species to which it belongs. In that way, one might fancifully say, dogs in general learn how to be dogs in increasing sufficiency. Only when an experience results from an exercise of free will does it become a part of the memory of the individual. The human physical structure, to take a simple example, is daily undergoing a great multitude of experiences having to do with the sensational and instinctive, and therefore automatic aspect of awareness – such things as the ordinary bodily functions. None of these experiences, so far as the individual is concerned, has any place in his final structure. But every experience which is a manner of action by free will, however slight, is drawn from that part of the cosmos which comprises the Not-done, and transferred into that part of the cosmos which comprises the Thing-done. The latter is, in the realest sense possible, a portion of the individual entity, *and will forever remain so*. The course of personal development, then, is a constant transferal from that which is outside in experience, permanently to that which is – not inside, but ourselves."

Another time one of us asked: "Is all evolution achieved by a process of assimilating experience? And is this assimilation an intellectual process?"

"Evolution," said the Invisible, "must, in the final analysis and in one way or another and at one time or another, pivot on an exercise of free will. Free will implies a decision, a choice between one thing, one course of action, one rejection or acceptance, and another. The mere experience and the mere translation into conscious possession are only the materials furnishing forth the opportunity for this exercise of free will. That which is absorbed but not intellectualized, and that which is intellectualized but not absorbed, are alike in that they are powerful in possibility but barren of result when viewed from the standpoint of personal evolution. In this regard they become significant only when they, or such portion of them as is appropriate to the moment, are utilized in decision or the exercise of free will."

Another time a little more detail was given us on the evolutionary process. On this occasion a friend who was a teacher was in a dilemma. He had been lectured by the Invisibles on the importance of balancing intake and outgo. How did this fit into the free-will-and-decision picture?

"The evolutionary process," said the Invisible, "for the teacher as for all others, is threefold – indivisibly threefold. Without adequate, balanced and complete working of all three aspects, futility results.

First, that which is to be given out is received, either through the spiritual senses or through unconscious experience of life. Next, it is understood intellectually by the focused mind – it is rationalized. This intellectualization can come about from within by constructive thought, or through recognition by means of something read or taught from outside. And third, the subject matter gains its dynamics.

"Now often the third element, that of obtaining dynamics, is omitted. As soon as the thing is intellectualized it is given out. That is the method of most teachers and preachers, polemic writers and reformers of the world. And because of the omission of the third essential, the effort is with little or no result.

"Dynamics are obtained only through the immersion of the concept in the substance of which your earth life is composed. That means it must be applied in the ordinary way of living to actual and constructive life. Only thus does it obtain a body of substance which will make it effective. The thing you learn and understand and become enthusiastic over and immediately give out as a teacher falls flat, because it is made, not of flesh and blood, but of an alien substance. The preacher who fills his church is the preacher who lives what he says outside his church. The teacher of influence is he who has bathed his ideas in life. And note the following: it is most important: this process of bathing in life is not a laboratory process; it is not a conscious bringing forth of doctrine for dipping in a solution prepared for the purpose; it is a taking the doctrine as part of yourself with you where you move among earth affairs. There are no preachers, there are no teachers, who are teachers and preachers only – not in the true sense of those terms. They are practitioners of life who bring from their daily uses their well-worn tools for explanation. He who learns must expand his practical earth life in equal measure to his learning, for his learning will in the long run equal his expansion."

— 3 —

We grow in consciousness, then, by making decisions. And the immediate product is individualized experience and memory.

Now one cannot make decisions that will result in experience without overt action. The action may be either mental or material, of course; though ordinarily the latter.

But it must be action, functioning. The wholly inert never progresses. So important and basic is this principle that for a long time our Invisibles hammered it at us, in its simplest form, over and over again. Only after the crude raw idea was integral to our thinking did they concede that the KIND of functioning had importance.

"It doesn't make the least difference what you do, which part of the world you choose to function in; it's the functioning itself that counts."

"What he means," another Invisible commented on this idea, "is, never mind whether or not you think your job is a fool job, if you know it's your job. But have no doubt as to that."

Or again:

"You can't find out anything by simply wondering. YOU have to get busy and do something. Just what you do does not really matter; it's the intention that counts. Perhaps you don't get that. I'll explain. You set about doing something. It goes flat. You try again. You quit. After a while you try again. Perhaps you never succeed, but the mere act of trying is sufficient to give you a sort of boost. Not a boost as respects that particular thing, but in a definite *direction*. On the other hand, if you lie down, you come to a dead stop. You have no momentum."

"Action is all of development," stated another Invisible. "Of course I do not necessarily mean physical action. The very first slight wee crawly movement on the part of the most microscopical creatures you can discern is not merely to insure the means of existence, though apparently that is the sole reason. The basic real reason is development-action. Any new thing must be acquired by action, by experience, before it can be told, either by you to yourself, or to you by somebody else. You can be *told* no new thing. You can be given the words, but you will not understand them. That's why there is so much vagueness and groping and dissatisfaction in the approach to anything new. You must first confront it, become aware that it exists. It is something; just *something*. You cannot understand it because you have no experience. Then you must act, and from the act, and its result, you get knowledge."

"But how about spiritual contact?" we asked. "You have been emphasizing how important that is, and the filling up at the Source. Now you seem to be trying to turn us back to the mere mechanism of daily life!"

"With the average man," observed the Invisible quaintly, "the building of a water wheel arouses an ambition to supply some water for it. He is proud of it and he wants to see it go."

— 4 —

As a corollary to this main theme, the Invisibles drew a fine distinction. It is only in functioning, they pointed out, that we experience reality at all. Things merely in relation one to the other are symbols of reality. In activity, in function, they become the *embodiment* of reality.

"As symbols," said our Invisible, "they merely stand for something behind them as a note on a page stands for a musical tone. A man in a world of physical objects, but static of emotions, actions, thoughts, is but surrounded by a multitude of suggestive symbols that stand for, but do not embody a reality remote from him. Through the symbols, and his imagination, he may surmise the existence of the reality. He may thus, to a certain extent, perhaps even manage a critical or appreciative understanding of it, but it will touch him only as a shadow touches the wall, leaving no impress. From it he obtains no experience of solid fact, but lives in a world of insubstantial poetry whose quality is that of dreams and whose endurance is as fleeting. If he is of mystic quality he is perpetually in anticipation of some remote time or state of existence when he shall break through the veil of illusion, as he calls it, to an undefined and rather vague reality of an unguessed form which he imagines to lie behind. He does not realize that in the nature of the universe, and under proper conditions, the reality enters into and informs with life the symbol itself – that the veil of illusion is itself illusion, and that, had he the secret, he could, with the fingers of his very own spirit, touch the living naked essence to which he longs so often in vain.

"To himself, each man is a reality; to himself he symbolizes nothing. He is, and in the mere fact of that being he touches an underlying fundamental essence of the real. This is simply and solely because the life that is in him functions. His appetites, his emotions, his passions, his imaginations, the coursing of his blood through his veins, the registration of light through his eyes, his movements and his every activity are not to him symbols, but are expressions of that which is his inner self, seeking outlet in a world of movement. The living intangibles flow through their respective mechanisms within him to produce, as far as his consciousness is concerned, a portion, limited though it may be, of absolute reality.

"But in the outer world, if he deprives himself, or is deprived, of acquired or natural-functioning correspondence with things about him, all things remain to him symbolical except himself, and he is surrounded by a dream world."

However, the argument can be turned inside out. Since the lack of function makes for the merely symbolic, the activity of function makes for reality.

"To the extent that man succeeds in functioning through that external world, he removes it from the category of symbols suggesting truth into the category of things conducting truth. Man's education and development on all planes of life and lives consists in his fashioning tools, skills, understandings and abilities actually to function in a wider and wider inclusion of his environment.

"Now the penalty for the fashioning of a tool is that it must be employed or it will rust. The obligation, then, of having developed correspondences, aptitudes, talents, skills, techniques, abilities to function, is their employment. Through them one translates the symbolical to the real; but, once the transmutation has taken place, a neglect to continue actually blunts the perceptions in that direction. In time, therefore, that particular thing will cease, not only to be a conductor of truth, but even to symbolize the truth, and so will end at last in something lifeless, useless. And dead things must be painfully carried away.

"So," the Invisible summed up, "a man should examine himself to see what he has learned to do, for what he has learned to do cries out for its fulfillment. In calling to life a need for the fulfillment of reality, he has to an extent chosen a road which he must tread out. Or if not a road, then certainly a direction. He has made himself tools that are his obligation of equipment. Possibly he may not use them in the way he intended when he fashioned diem, but use them he must – if he is to continue in the realm of reality."

To test our grasp of the principle the Invisible asked that one of us repeat back the gist as we understood it. One of us did so.

"If an ability has been called into being as a transmuting and expressing channel for some form of reality, the individual is subsequently obligated to continue and fulfill the obligation so undertaken, or its complete equivalent in some other form."

"Yes," agreed the Invisible, "but I would state it a bit differently. The fashioning of a tool by means of which one functions in a symbol to transmute it to a reality, imposes an obligation to continue that transmutation *in one form or another*. It is permissible to discard that tool only when by means of some other tool the same transmutation is continued. Now beware," he warned, "lest too-close inspection of a very large and general law gets you to splitting hairs of literal interpretation. There is, of course room for experiment and room for expanding in new interests."

The teaching just given does not mean that one must stick to a thing merely because he has begun it. That would be perilously close to a philosophy of drudgery. And if there is one thing these Invisibles of ours had no use for at all, it is drudgery.

"If you find you have made a mistaken choice in some specific activity," said they, "remember it is not a fatal and divorceless marriage. But," they added emphatically, "it will be necessary to determine what reality has been transmuted, and the old task must not be abandoned until an equal transmutation is assured in another direction. Be it noted," they pointed out, "genuine mistakes rarely result in a very high order of transmutation anyway. What we are warning about is abandonment without sufficient cause, from whim."

— **5** —

One of our group had an idea. How about functions that had been carried through to their full perfection? Does there then remain, as far as the individual is concerned, an obligation to continue to employ them? Or are they then outgrown, as is the vermiform appendix? "Is there," be expressed it, "anything to the oriental notion that we outgrow any

44

function by perfecting and rounding out its manifestation?

"Cart before the horse," answered the Invisible. "You do not use a function in order to perfect it; you perfect a function in order to use it. Its best use begins when it has been perfected – that would be a silly time to discard it. Your generalization is as though you were to recommend a violinist to work until thoroughly satisfied with his technique – and then to consider his job done and smash his violin! Functions are indeed occasionally to be discarded, but as a rule only because you have perfected a better tool; or because you are actually, though perhaps not evidently, otherwise doing the same activity."

"It seems to me," suggested the inquirer, "you might sometimes grow into different needs, and hence require different mechanisms to fulfill the new needs."

"And perhaps discard the old one which has fulfilled its need," supplemented the Invisible. "In your earth, however," he added, "it is a rare thing thus to discard a function. Its seeming disappearance merely means that it has been refined to correspond to a higher and finer-grain aspect of the same activity."

"A transmutation of energy to a higher form by the disintegration of a lower form," came a further suggestion from us.

"Transformation, not disintegration," corrected the Invisible, "a sublimation."

The last word led to a passing consideration of the withdrawal-into-monasteries idea which was one of the ideals of the Middle Ages. The Invisible was against it – at least, for us.

"Every person should recognize the necessity for living a normal active life, and not be longing for the next world. Now, have you ever understood why, if all this we have told you be true, it has not been sooner revealed and more widely understood – and why, even today, so few people really comprehend? Because it is too strong meat for most. Because it is liable to take your mind away from the job that belongs to you. That's why. But: you *can* take it intellectually and not emotionally, and that is the very way you should take it. You must know the reality of the continuity of the entity, and in understanding that you must understand that you are given a span on earth in which to live on EARTH, worthily, so you may take on immortality in the hereafter. Every man is an individual entity. He is responsible for that. You have been given free will, the greatest gift in the entire universe. Now you live up to it! And how can you do it by gazing off and not doing the job?"

"How about the ancient saints?" asked one of us. "They seemed to have what might be called subjective functioning, without apparent objective correspondences. Was this abnormal?"

"That depends. To the extent to which they consciously functioned according to their own stage of development they were normal. To the extent to which they were seeking their soul's salvation, or their own ecstasy, they were not. Only such rare entities as the few who have lived earth life possessed of nearly complete earthly development can successfully or usefully attempt a purely subjective life on the earth plane. With others it smacks somewhat of both conceit and arrogance, for it is an assumption either that they have already completed the earth job, or that they know enough and are privileged enough to step aside from the ordered scheme. The only road to the subjective life, as you call it, is by the steps of accomplishment in the environment in which you are placed. That is why you are placed there rather than somewhere else.

"Do not misunderstand. In ordinary spiritual contact there may be a feeling that you describe as ecstasy. I use the term in its mystic sense of tingling high pleasure, as in the communion of the nuns and monks and that type. He who carries this ecstasy eventually through the formulation period into manifestation of one sort or another, is functioning in the normal course. It might be so that one can receive from universal consciousness direct, but he cannot render back to universal consciousness by any other way than external manifestation. He cannot effectively face upstream and barrenly return towards the source merely an emotion, however elevating and satisfactory that may seem.

"Anything normally functioning produces an emotion of pleasure; the pleasure is oft of a type and intensity commensurate with the breadth and depth and cosmic significance of the function. The highest emotional content must be in the perfect functioning. The pleasure is legitimately enjoyed to its thrill of rapture so long as it is a concomitant of function and does not become an end in itself. The proper action of any major function implies the proportionate functioning of any subordinate function. Can you not see, then, that a neglect of one or more lesser functions, because you get pleasure in a larger function, immediately implies the pursuit of the pleasure for itself? It therefore becomes a perversion, as sometimes in the case of the monastic ecstasy before mentioned."

"I am warned to go no further in this, as it can but give a false impression. The very word 'function' is itself too heavy-footed to follow the subtle, flexible and delicate reality. 'As a man thinks, so he does' is true, but a better saying is 'as a man does, so will he eventually think,' when leaden-footed thought has overtaken."

— 6 —

Function, then, is the very basis of all evolution. And the key to *individual* evolution is decision. So don't get the habit of letting others make your decisions for you.

"Individual development," said the Invisible, "is a matter of decision. Even a mistaken decision may result in considerable advancement. You move by making your mistaken decisions or your happy choices, as the case may be."

"Decision," another agreed, "is the vital principle of individual progress, and cannot be taken out of the individual's hands without a far-reaching harm.

"By making a person's decision for him you have deprived him of a certain opportunity and therefore a certain property. You have robbed him, even with the best intentions in the world. He may thereby gain certain easements unearned, but at the same time he has been forced to forego a chance for certain self-building which the process of earning would have accomplished for him."

The Invisibles were constantly recurring to the point; it was of supreme importance. To a visitor who asked for specific advice, they had this to say:

"I would not steal from you. You are in a world with just so many opportunities of choice, of right choice and wrong choice, just so many unique opportunities for learning from the results of your choices. Therefore, we have called it a selective world in which you are placed ultimately to determine what is worth and what is not worth the choosing. In this one particular respect your earth life is more richly endowed than any other phase of existence you will probably be called upon to pass through. Each time you allow another to determine for you what is within your own choice, you have allowed that man to dip his hand into your pocket and take from you a bit of property you cannot replace. You would think hardly of a friend who took from you gold pieces. I am your friend, and I would not take from you what is more precious than gold. So I shall not answer those questions."

And similarly, to a similar request on another occasion:

"Would you thank anyone who was to take from you an opportunity to make money? Why should you thank us for taking from you a legitimate and never-repeatable opportunity for progress? It will not come again. If that moment is taken away from you, you are that much poorer for all eternity. You may steal a man's purse, and you can make restitution. But if you steal a man's opportunity for making a decision, you take that which you can never return to him. Each decision made is a step in your development, a moment in your eternity. Once passed, it is gone forever."

IV The Positive Ingredient

I CAN just suggest the truth by the fragrance of it.
BETTY

— **1** —

FUNCTIONING means more than mere activity. For complete fulfillment it must have one certain positive content. Otherwise it is at best a purposeless stirring about, and at worst deadening drudgery. There is nothing intrinsic to any form of activity that makes it one thing or the other. Any business whatever with which we may concern ourselves may be either constructive functioning or drudgery. That depends not at all on what the thing is in itself. I once knew a man who was enthusiastic as a garbage collector, and had a half-dozen good reasons. Indeed anything can be transformed from drudgery to real functioning. The change needs only one ingredient.

Drudgery is something which must be done, and we seem to be the ones to do it, so we do it. But it exhausts us. Why? Because we are not interested. Interest is the missing ingredient; what Betty called eagerness, zest.

That is all very well to say, but how can one pump up zest for a repeated daily routine intrinsically not only uninteresting, but a deadly bore? Like washing the dishes; or slugging away on a production line? It is silly and hypocritical and posey and a pretense to pump up any artificial enthusiasm for that kind of a job.[*]

"True," the Invisibles acknowledged. "Of course you cannot go around zesting things priggishly. What we must get into this is naturalness, not priggishness."

Cannot be done? The Invisibles deny that.

"Nothing," they stated emphatically, "is too small to work on with the tools of spiritual values. Take the smallest things, little hourly experiences or situations of a commonplace day; you can, by your concentration of desire, transfer them into a spiritual significance akin to a poem. You can even take a nap with a spark of interest, instead of just a dead exhausted failing away.

"The joke of it is," interposed Betty, "there is a trick about doing it; and the trick is to enjoy the doing. You haven't found the real secret, unless you've found that. I know this isn't new; but it's going to be said over and over and over again, until it acquires the same importance in life as eating tomorrow's dinner. We are sure to feed ourselves that way! "

— **2** —

A clue to accomplishing this was given us later in the distinction between two types of impelling force. They called them will-power and desire-power. Will-power they here used in the narrower sense of driving forward against reluctance or inertia; something dragging or even disagreeable. There is of course a

_____

[*] See *Anchors to Windward* for a fuller exposition of this idea.

wider sense to the word, but that was aside from their present purpose.

"There is," said they, "always a contracted and expanded form to everything. Will-power is the contracted form of this higher thing. You can step into it from will-power without contracting, if you think of it as *desire-power*. Will-power is in spite of your preference, doubling the pressure. Will-power is a faculty of holding yourself up. This other is a power of outreaching yourself by desire."

"It is the great secret of power," commented Betty. "I can see it work over and over again. It's a process of making pleasurable your will-power. The minute you make it pleasurable it starts working, like a chemical affinity, pumping warmer vitality into your object, making it work itself naturally. What a nice secret! It's a process of work. It doesn't matter what it is – playing tennis or growing into life."

"I want you," said the Invisible, "to substitute for the stiff words 'will-power' the same idea in a natural exuberance of appropriating life."

And on another occasion:

"Consider the directing power of one's self. Do not stiffen the idea with the rigidity of the words 'will-power.' Do not leave out the warm fostering condition of heartily and enthusiastically *desiring* to accomplish. That contains the secret of success, the diagnosis of failure. One should bring to bear on it the same simple attitude of mind with which one approaches one's vacation days, one's hobby, one's favorite Interest, either of work or of play. People often work so hard at play. Lightness in living – that's play, isn't it? Don't let living be heavy. Reorganize it and keep it light.

"We must get the whole of this force," said Betty, "not merely the detached bits we recognize in the words 'will-power.' Lifting-power is what I am trying for. What is that big thing? Oh, we haven't scratched the surface with words! We've dimly sensed the urge in a snail-like thing we call evolution, the lowest speed, dragging gait of progress. That isn't the way it's meant to be: this other thing is the way it's meant to be. In evolution the power is barely great enough to drag us along. This way we go with it.

"All we seem to realize is that will-power accomplishes certain results of self-propulsion. But look how hard you run in tennis, or walk in fishing or doing something you like. That's another sort of self-propulsion: easier because you are in *harmony with what you are doing*. That isn't generally recognized as part of the lifting force. And it gets so stiff and painful when you do it from the will-power side. This whole fabric of lifting-power is quite new to me. It's so definitely divorced from the mind: will-power is centered in the mind. Mind is the planning organ. But that which carries out the plans of the mind is the real executive. This force is to will-power what will-power is to the mind. I don't know what that real executive of you is called. There's a lift to happiness and harmony which is so much easier a way than this painful will-power business. It makes the leaping flame instead of just a smolder. One is done with your united being; and the other in spite of your divided being."

Much later Betty out of her experience of the

moment coined a significant phrase.

"Had a nice *combustion of happiness*," said she. "It revealed something to me. There's a great big principle there.

This morning in my shower, when I turned it from warm to cold, I thought, Ha! here comes the cold! I'll grapple with it and exercise myself against it! You old cold, you; I'll show you! Ha! And that element of pleasure in meeting it enthusiastically, and outdistancing it, as it were, was a discovery. I enjoyed it, and was warm under it without feeling bitten by it... I can't tell it. Anyhow, I know there's a *dynamo in enthusiastic combustion.*"

— 3 —

Later on the Invisibles defined the positive ingredient more clearly. Then we understood why they had stepped around it so carefully. It calls for a word which has become, as Betty said, a "skiddy word." This one certainly needs retreading, for there is no substitute that carries the whole meaning. The word is *love*. It is a pity we cannot discard its sickly sentimental connotations and use it in its fresh and simple meaning.

"The word," said the Invisibles, "has become a palimpsest overlaid with the scribblings of many interpreters until the original simple writing has been obscured. But this is true: whatever is done, whether in the physical world, in human relations, in the substance of thought, or spiritual contact – whatever is done with LOVE endures. All else is consumed in the eventual transformation. I do not mean necessarily and completely 'sentimental' love. If I were to attempt, in a

55

few words, to define what I mean, I'd say *'things done heartily'* – these alone have a complete and ultimate influence in the accretion and the fashioning of the spirit entity.

"Love comprises all that is of a positive character. It is understanding as well as sentiment. But it has many ingredients, and all must be equally developed before perfect love is attained. Any effort, any outward-looking thing that constructs is an ingredient of love. The man who builds conscientiously a brick wall is manifesting one of the ingredients of love. It is of course a small ingredient as compared to what is manifested when a man sacrifices his life for another."

— **4** —

How – or where – can one acquire more of this "love"? If it is the foundation of all individual progress, and if we happen to be deficient in it, we are in a bad way. The, answer, technically, is complex, as will appear later in these pages. But we can get a glimpse from a talk we had with Betty, long after, when she was in the unobstructed universe.

"There are," said she, "in your obstructed universe, three kinds of love: sacrificial love; demanding love; and the third – I'm troubled for my adjective. It's the combination of the other two: it enfolds."

"Interfusing love?" one of us proposed.

"It's more than that."

"Describe its action. That may suggest something."

"Well," said Betty, "demanding love includes the need of expressions of love. Limited-universe marriage is part that. Also work – a man's love for his work. Ambition, too. It's laudable.

"Sacrificial love – true mother's love is frequently just that. Patriotism. Self-denial. Wide charity.

"All love is good, but the third love is above, higher – *edits* the other two. It encompasses; it knows. It knows how far sacrifice should go, how far demands should go. The source – they who have this love in your universe have tapped the source. It is inclusive; it contains the other two, and their expressions. It radiates above and beyond the emotion of human relationships, yet it includes them. It enfolds and *comprehends*, though sometimes without individual *understanding* on your plane of the universe. That is the love that Christ talked about, and it includes all the gradations, glories, and beauties of the other two."

"Could be called the state of love?" one of us queried.

"Yes. The reason for this rather academic discussion of love is that I want to create in your consciousness the reality of the entity of love. One of the miscomprehended statements of Biblical literature is this: God is love.

"Now that 'state of love' is the third kind. It is

one of the most important facts of the unobstructed universe. Love, if I can use an analogy, is so actual here with us that it needs no more factual assurance than the air you breathe. Love with me is so real that I can permeate you with it. I enfold you. I make you conscious of it – or rather if you accept it you will be conscious of it. You don't need to ask for it, you don't need to demand it, because it is always there. You just HAVE it. Now all individuality has to have a focus, a peg on which to hang itself. I am your peg. But you can so love me that this love permeates all of your own universe and carries over to ours – bridges."

"Could not too exclusive a focus on the peg be detrimental to the wide aspect?" I asked.

"If it is only the demanding love."

And here is another side-glimpse from another Invisible at another time.

"All love, from the love of a flower or a bit doggie or even a skyline by a hill, to the love between two human beings, is nought whatever but an unrecognized realization, not merely of kinship, but of actual identity. It is a fragment, not yet intellectualized, of what will be in the course of development a universal, and not a fragmentary thing. Love may be defined in terms of identity, just as, in dealing with particulars, identity may be defined in the terms of love. They are interchangeable terms."

V Negatives

THE ultimate aim, in the highest utilization of any material environment such as your earth, is the fullest expression of spirit in the completest manifestation of matter.

INVISIBLE

STRAIN will never accomplish anything but defeat. If radiance were anything but illumination in rapture, it would not be radiance.

INVISIBLE

— **1** —

WE HAVE touched on the positive side of function. There is also to be examined the negative side, the reverse of eagerness. And that is fairly well expressed by what the Invisibles called "drab-colored words" – drudgery and duty.

Now here, the Invisibles acknowledge, might be preached what could readily be made into dangerous doctrine. That is, if it is taken as sanction to license or avoidance. It is neither, as you will see when you have finished this chapter, nor is it in any manner relief from responsibility.

Even though that is understood, the two proposals are startling enough at first glance.

Never be content to pursue a course of action

merely because it is your "duty."

Never "give up" things for the sake of your soul.

— 2 —

Over the years these two admonitions were given us many times without great elaboration. But when the Invisibles finally tackled the subject in detail they began with general principles.

"The more fully," said they, "you can live outwardly and inwardly expressed, and develop the thing that is individually and personally and uniquely you, the more completely are you fulfilling function. But the deep-set currents of your being are not always easy to recognize. Do not mistake the ghostly pressures of habit, of environment, of the power of old-time thought. They are strong in conviction. Naked duty is easy to mark as the flint-faced hag she is. But clothed in tradition and the expectation of approval or reward she often hides her identity. Always remember that a thing done merely because it is a conventional duty, unbacked by the essence of self, is sterile and unproductive. There is no duty to others that is not also a duty to one's self.

"It is for this reason we have so often deprecated the value of plain and gray duty. It is even seriously to be doubted whether one should ever be content merely to 'do his duty.' If it appears to him as a duty, with a capital D, then he is regarding that event too superficially. He must lay aside that particular aspect which shows itself as a duty, and go back and back of it until he finds something wider and more inclusive, which he can perform heartily. For example, one is a wee lad and he looks with considerable disfavor on a long wet tramp through the brae to bring homeward the kine, and he goes forth for the performance of that task only because he feels it to be his duty. If this lad is a Scot, and hence philosophically inclined, he might conceivably be able to abandon the thought of the task as a duty and obtain a necessary enthusiasm to make of it a formative thing – and these little things are formative as well as the big things – by reflecting on the real pleasure it will give his widowed mother to see him taking responsibility. Thus he has centered his force of motivation not in the detail of the thing to be done, but in a wider underlying principle. This is a crude childish illustration, but I purposely take the very simplest example to make clear what I mean. No man should ever merely 'do his duty'; but in recognizing a duty as such, he should examine back and back of it to find it is only one detail of a larger principle which is his pleasure. If he cannot do that he must not do his duty. I speak here, of course, as you understand, in a rather exaggerated hyperbole. It is sometimes desirable to do certain drudgeries which cannot be avoided, pending the discovery of the leaven which will make them palatable.

"Indeed, such performances are often valuable, as callisthenic exercises are valuable, in strengthening spiritual muscles. But it must not be thought for a moment that one is thereby attaining grace, as so many worth-while people imagine. The disagreeable, merely as such, is never constructive in the direct sense. The disagreeable, however, is often a challenge to our spiritual perceptions. Unless the thing presented for our performance is evil or out of harmony, there exists in it somewhere – if our natures are developed enough to find it – an aspect or an inclusion which will fit into our world of things done heartily. All life is a challenge to our spiritual perception of harmony – there is nothing but what fits if only we can find out how."

– 3 –

This brings us to the question of sacrifice, and especially self-sacrifice. In popular esteem, sacrifice is meritorious. We admire it, though we may not do it. And we tend to look on it as a moral duty. There is that "duty" again. But the Invisibles had other ideas.

"Self sacrifice," said they, "in the popular conception of giving up your own to another almost indiscriminately and without reference to the conditions, is often bad. It may indicate merely laziness or a vain self-righteousness. Self-sacrifice, so called, is true and constructive only when it has its inception in the field of complete inner conviction. And then it is merely a recognition, conscious or intuitive, of the fact that the harmonious need of the moment is for relinquishment. And since this is a natural process, it is in final analysis a joyous process, as is any harmonious functioning.

"A man should not give up an object of desire because of some rigid intellectual idea of duty, or some weak sentiment or emotion, or some mistaken conception of stripping himself to give to others as a meritorious thing in itself. He should relinquish only because he senses that the occasion demands, for the harmony of which he is a part, a foregoing rather than an insistence. In this understanding, what the world calls self-sacrifice is no sacrifice at all, in the sense that it involves much pain or ultimate regret.

"Indeed, if pain is felt in arriving at the point of relinquishment, he can always apply a sure test. This test is whether, through the decision at which he has arrived, he experiences a completely unregretful satisfaction and a sense of having done the totally harmonious thing. If still there lingers a strong sense of mere duty, that in itself indicates that he has not functioned entirely within his field of complete understanding.

"Sometimes his decision, from an abstract point of view, may be intrinsically correct, and he 'should' make the sacrifice. Nevertheless, from his personal point of view the struggle to be made is not in the direction of this especial relinquishment. It is within himself, to extend his understanding so that it will include the pressure which has forced him to the decision of mere duty.

"Or, again, it may be that his duty decision is intrinsically wrong, though he may not know it. To give up what he should defend may throw confusion into the harmony of the General Plan. Knowingly to abandon to others that which is not their right may only deprive him of that which he should rightfully have. At the same time it may also fill unhealthily a gap whose completion by effort should have developed certain qualities in the others.

"You must not forget that in such decisions all your powers – intellectual, emotional, intuitional – must be accorded full play. If a man comes to such a decision without calling upon himself fully, he may permit surface desirabilities too great an importance. He may penetrate so little beyond his mere liking as never to allow other influences access to him. Perhaps, when he goes deeper into himself, he may discover that in these particular circumstances he may not like these things at all! – however desirable they may be in other and perhaps more ordinary circumstances. Then his feet are on the ground."

— **4** —

Most of us think of asceticism as the supreme example of self-sacrifice. Likewise most of us harbor a sneaking suspicion that there may be some sort of good in it. The Invisibles would have none of this.

"It is a mistaken idea," said they, "that conscientious and ritualistic giving up of things has merit. Giving up things, per se, has no merit at all. The moment any philosophy, any system of thought denies or avoids, you may know that it is wrong. Perhaps you may have to search for meanings and adjustments and proportions before your life will work smoothly, but you cannot cut off part of it and have anything left but a monstrosity. That is the trouble with all asceticisms. The idea is not to divest yourself but to utilize yourself; to express the whole of yourself and not just a part. Welcome and accept all human instincts, all savoring of life. No matter how commonplace, how humble or capable of being used solely for material purposes certain functions may be – nevertheless, properly viewed, properly utilized, each may express some aspect of spirit that otherwise could not be as adequately expressed."

Objection to this doctrine occurred to us. For a good many centuries, we pointed out, the school of monasticism, withdrawal, abstinence, denial has had great authority and unassailable standing as the way to spiritual life. As one of us phrased it, "the oriental retirement from the trivialities of ordinary life in order to concentrate on spiritual growth."

"The product of that system," said the Invisible, "is not without value. Nevertheless, it does not fulfill the ideal of its functioning. It is too thoroughly an individualistic achievement. It lacks the contagious quality which should make it avail in the common earth life. Whatever its reachings, its powers and its appeals, they are primarily adapted to other planes than that of physical earth, and may only, by art and knowledge, be secondarily applied to the earth plane.

"I must repeat: no physical aspect of life, no matter how unlikely it may seem at first glance, but has a spiritual complement which its use, or indulgence, can release. The task of the world is to find and to grow into these correspondences. The long spiritual striving of the East fell into negations and avoidances. So it has attenuated itself into what might be called a sterile and solitary functioning, mostly on a plane not intended in the original plan. It is necessary, then, to start anew in the richness of the soil."

The idea of asceticism, the Invisibles hastened to add, is by no means peculiar to the East. Indeed the West, especially in the Dark Ages, carried it to the extreme of fanaticism with only a minimum of the wider spiritual connotations.

"Christianity likewise fell into negation," said the Invisible, "and in a manner even more fatal than in the case of the Eastern beliefs. The negations of the latter were at least motivated by the theory that they were an integral element of higher growth. The negations of the West, however, came to their authority merely through a constricting fear, so that in their final form they implied that aught of earth that gave pleasure must, by that very fact, be deterrent. This peculiar doctrine took its inception from an eager instinct for concentration, and a mistaken extension of the primitive rite of sacrificial offering. It was a sublimation, in a way, of the old savage superstition that the sacrifice of that which the suppliant holds dear is a propitiation for ultimate favor. In primitive society the sacrifice of a bullock was made to win immediate privilege from a personal god. In the larger later development the sacrifice was of those things that made life pleasurable, in order to purchase a remote and future 'heaven.' So sublimated, there increasingly became attached to it a body of inhibition which, in aggregate, made indeed of earth existence a 'vale of tears,' supportable only as a price of future, and otherwise unearned, bliss.

"Unfortunately this attitude is still very common. It varies widely in degree and gets startlingly diverse results. To it are due a great list of prohibitions, ranging from the imposed celibate orders to the keeping of the Sabbath holy by reducing its activities to the smallest trickle that could sustain life. All this diversity could, however, be comprised again in that single, dry-rotting word, negation. In place of transforming ever more and more of the functions of material life into their proper expression of the complementary spiritual values, the process tends rather to wither more and more even of the significances already in existence. As a consequence this Western philosophy, like the Eastern, has become a dead-end product, without further growth. Both will continue to function, each in its own way, but in the future their contribution must be rather that of the tributary than that of the main current.

"The task of your evolution is not to deny, for all negation is either deterrent or destructive. The real task is to utilize and educate, so that your action may not only fully and pleasurably express all its earthly capabilities, but also act as a conduit to its appropriate spiritual counterpart. There is no thing, no function, no pleasure, no gratification but can in development not only express its first and obvious earthly content, but also be made to release its complementary spiritual content. Your part is to live in full, as far as you may, all correspondences that your material earth presents to you; to do so without negation; but so to accept and use each and every one of them that you may eventually discern and attract its spiritual meaning. This is not only a satisfying, but an immensely thrilling pursuit. You exercise in it the instinct and ingenuity, not of your mind but of your heart. And when that spiritual complement is finally uncovered by you, sometimes in the most unexpected and unlikely aspects, you will experience the excitement and satisfaction of one who at once discovers and enriches. That use and that meaning are in every natural aspect of your earth life. The future of the general spiritual advance of your race is dependent upon this process of discovery. As an individual you contribute your quota of your personal research, for that research is synonymous with growth. In this plowing and fallow time, when it seems the race lives in a muck of materialism, that is the harrowing you may contribute. It is in the muck because it begins a fresh and, we hope, more glorious attempt."

Still, we were not satisfied.

"How about the so-called Masters of the Far East," we wanted to know. "If they attained to their advanced powers by withdrawing to the Himalayas and doing Yogi exercises, then why shouldn't we?"

"You have the thing wrong end to," replied the Invisible." John Jones could not withdraw to the Himalayas and do the things in the certain way you speak of and become an adept. It is only an adept who can do it. It is not by conscious taking of thought, and withdrawing from life for the purpose of pursuing spirituality like an elusive and rather solitary fox, that one attains – unless the withdrawal seems, not a question, but the most natural thing in the world. An effort to renounce is not the effort which is the price of all growth. The effort must be always to expand, to reach out, to gain more contacts, to live everyday life with a leaven of sympathy, and to walk on the highest plane of which one is capable. If these things are done naturally and simply and eagerly and with a will, spirituality, as you call it, will flood in, bringing with it all its gifts of intuition, of spiritual wisdom, of cosmic contact. But that is a thing which must be left to take care of itself. All the other is yours to do, and to its doing you bring all that you can of that which comes to you on the flood."

– 5 –

These pronouncements, I realize, will strike many as radical and iconoclastic. But not many of the younger generation. Outgrowing things is their specialty. Nevertheless, there are two sides to the picture.

"The younger generation's overturning of our lifeless idols of duty and sacrifice," said the Invisible, "is in reality a very healthy rebellion. The farther reaches of psychology have showed the damaging impress of these older concepts. Now, what the younger generation have not discovered yet – life will surely teach them – is the seeing the scheme of responsibility whole. They must realize their importance in the creative scheme of things, so that the unquestioned giving of themselves to doing their part is as healthy an outgoing of self as a good football tackle. The seeing of their responsibilities whole will finally reveal duty and sacrifice, in their essential structure, as full-blooded essentials of conquest rather than old dried mummies of dogma.

"These young rebels are the creative ones or the next generation. But they will find they can't work successfully without a technique of association. And they haven't gone far enough yet to build themselves a better and healthier one than the old.

"What they'll find in time is that the job can't be done, however improved their new tools may be, without the *essentials* of duty and sacrifice. But they must get them in their own terms, and the result won't be the old thing at all. Enthusiasm will be its life blood."

VI Conscious Development

IT IS HARD for us to foresee here what will be the results of this more general belief and how much we dare reveal. The teachers are all very cautious, for reaction must be carefully reckoned before knowledge can be given out. There is so much danger in the present situation that it is one of the first things we are cautioned about, when we are allowed to give communications: that is to be very watchful and not go too far, to move slowly and cautiously for the present. We have to note results carefully. It is the most intensive and comprehensive campaign that has ever been arranged over here, they say. It will be the most far-reaching and we are all tremendously excited about it. You see, we are under strict orders and have to evade sometimes the way they do on a witness stand, because we are not quite sure how much we dare tell. Also there is great care taken lest any conflicting information gets out. It is a wonderfully well-planned campaign. There is great consultation here all the time and we have to report results of our work... I am aching to tell you lots more state secrets, but I cannot. Don't forget one thing, will you? and that is that a wonderful age of stimulated creation is ahead, the result of the war suffering. We are all watching so eagerly the growth of the big things.

INVISIBLE

DON'T You imagine that, if a seed could think, it might look on you as spirits with the wisdom of God, because you made it grow by cultivation and the understanding of law? Well, suppose yourselves seeds underground, and think of us as ordinary people who have a higher comprehension of law, and who help you germinate.

INVISIBLE

— 1 —

WE PROCEED in evolution by expansion of consciousness. This takes place through function by the natural processes of growth. But when the time is ripe for the individual, he may greatly foster – not force – the natural process by taking conscious charge. Before that ripe moment he is more or less insulated from spiritual awareness, ordinarily, by indifference or open skepticism. That is why revelation – any revelation, great or small – generally receives limited acceptance. That is why pressure methods and proselytizing have so little permanent value. Per contra, when the moment of ripeness does arrive the opportunity is always there. Whether it comes in one form or another does not matter. There are many forms, and as many approaches.

The moment of ripeness comes to races as well as individuals. Then we find especial effort on the part of the invisible powers. There is a surge of interest and effort and belief. Sometimes this is expressed in material or economic or political terms; sometimes in what is known as "psychics," or intellect, or religion.

Apparently the present is one of those moments. The plowing and harrowing of war and social disturbances have prepared both general conditions and the individual for a fresh sowing. And through suffering the fields of human thinking have been made receptive.

"This," said the Invisibles, "is the most marvelously plastic time we shall have for eons. For that reason it is vitally important to utilize it. We are all of us making a mold. Youth feels it most; feels the healthy intuition to go as far as possible in freedom, to outrun the greatest possible distance from the old shackles, now, while it is possible, before the stiffening process begins again.

"Whispered counsels, too low to be heard by the world of ruder comprehension, have kept alive the mere trace of spiritual consciousness which exists today. Now the effort is to the fostering of development of this nearly lost potentiality. You can see for yourself, when you contemplate the historical picture, how necessary it has been to bring to earth the scientific strength, control and rationale of physical law. But, now that it bids fair to topple over its own structure by limiting satisfactions to its own achievements, it must regain impetus by directing its explorations to new fields, illuminating hitherto unseen possibilities."

"It looks," observed Betty, "like the last lap of a period in time which is ripening a movement. There is a confident feeling that we need only wait so long – it is not very long – before a new epoch comes in. I am delighted with the looks of it. What a comfort it will be to have everybody hang their own responsibilities on *themselves* through their own standards of belief! It can only be done by waiting for the maturity of this idea, this level of belief they are growing. There are a few here and there who stand out above the others, but it must be an accepted thing by the majority before it can do the race much good...

"I wonder what that nice new shining idea is? It has so much vitality. I can see it springing out of laboratories, out of books, leaping and bounding into life...

"Nothing is as important for this particular age.

He says that distinctly. No inventions or peerless presentations of any form of human conceptions are as important as personal demonstration of the harmonious living which comes of spiritual consciousness. It is a great message, to those who are prepared, to go forth into the world as lawgivers of life, healers and harmonizers, inspirers and gift bringers from the wider, freer, bolder life. They called me to say it, but I'm not good enough to translate. That's too bad. But perhaps even in dusty fragments the message may have some beauty, though it hardly seems possible. There's nothing anybody can do so important as to gain the consciousness of hourly spiritual influence."

— **2** —

The time is ripe, then, for many of us to take conscious charge of our development. It hardly needs saying that conscious contribution has the potentiality of being many times more effective than any blind offering – for good or for ill. But how do we go about this taking over? In the telling, the answer is deceptively simple: by conscious cooperation with spiritual forces. Even in the dawnings of understanding, mankind had a dim appreciation of this. We call that appreciation by the general term "religion." Crude as it originally was, adulterated as it always has been by selfish and material ends, nevertheless it had in it always an element of true spiritual cooperation. And in certain historical instances it became almost pure spirit offering itself up in service of the All.

Meantime the work of the world had to be done. So insistent is that necessity that it is probably a good thing the average man still does not see clearly what it is all about. The job has to be done. We can take no chances that it may be dropped in favor of a mistaken pursuit of Higher Powers.

Here we must return once more to our aim. All along we have seen that our basic obligation is self-development. But before we pursue that obligation into spiritual realms it behooves us to ask ourselves a question. For what purpose do we seek to further ourselves in evolution? What is our private aim in this seeking? Is it ourselves as ourselves? Or have we a more inclusive purpose?

In this connection let us examine the other aspect of the twofold objective of evolution. You will recall this as the coordination of individuals in a functioning Unity. Later, in defining education, this was expressed differently as "the process of changing the emphasis from the egocentric to the altruistic." Including this aspect, then, our own basic aim is to *make of ourselves agents better equipped to aid in the advance of the whole.*

In the larger sense that which subserves the universal Aim is good – whatever it is. That which does not subserve it is evil – whatever it is. In judging, therefore, whether our reaching out for spiritual forces is Right or Wrong, we may ignore the bewilderments of detailed method, provided we Are wholeheartedly honest in our basic aim – to make of ourselves agents better equipped to aid in the advance of the whole. In this, as in all enterprise, we can rely absolutely on the sure protection that, if our aim is single and pure, we are safe. If it is diluted with self-seeking – in the narrower sense – or with pride, then we are in danger. The matter is as simple as that. Above I with pride. The moment we begin to look upon our efforts toward spiritual cooperation as placing us above others in an "especially selected" category, then we enter a blind alley. Apropos, it would be well to re-examine the beatitudes through retranslation from the Aramaic. The same symbol that indicates "spirit" in that language means also "pride." "Blessed are the poor in spirit" is rather too humble; "blessed are the poor in pride" really means something.

How are we to judge whether or not our aim is pure? Is there any compass we can steer by? The answer is yes. It is the results of our efforts as reflected in our lives. What direction do our actions take, naturally and without strain?

At this point we must use another word that needs retreading. All down the years mankind has used it to mark an ultimate goal. As with all such fundamental terms, it has become overlaid with the partial and the sentimental and the false. I refer to the word "service." This has been so abused that to many it has become a cause for levity or cynicism. When it was offered to Betty she did not like it. But it caused her to find another, of an allied nature. One we shall return to later in these pages.

"Service is a cold word," she objected; "this is a warm, living – a sort of spontaneous creation, a curiously spreading, outgoing thing. It is more like production through the desire to produce. I can't see much of this strain and duty and uninspired effort, heaviness of work which I, and everyone else, go through to accomplish things. There is something one-sided when it's that way. This other is like the hard work you do in play, only it's a consuming, quickening, life-begetting thing. It is glowing, pulsing, sweeping you along. We weren't meant to work with heaviness; it's a discordant condition. Work is just fun. What a pity that the tradition of work has become so painful. Work! Production. Work is painful: production is better. Service has a sterile taint. What can I get that is self-acting? Creation is the nearest to it. That is a cleaner, brighter word. People do not create under a lash."

Creativeness, then, is the test we are looking for. If our lives are creative, in the inclusive sense of contributing something real to humanity, then we are on the right track.

— **3** —

There are a thousand methods of cooperating consciously with spiritual forces, ranging from performing the most humdrum tasks with a full content of spiritual understanding to the most profound philosophical or religious undertaking – and everything in between. It is a mistake to suppose that spiritual growth must be technical. That our own approach happened to be the psychic means nothing as a prescription. It is a road for specialists, and is one of the more dangerous ways unless skillfully and continuously safeguarded. The safeguard is, again, the aim. For what reason is one doing it? For development of psychic stunts and powers? For material benefit? For personal pride or prestige? Out of curiosity? Or for the single purpose of becoming a better tool?

At the risk of tiresome repetition I must reiterate that there is in everything, in every activity, this potential duality of purpose. The most clearly defined illustrations can be cited in the professions. A young man "expands his consciousness" in medical school to acquire skill to heal. His primary ambition may be to bring ease to suffering, or it may be a fashionable practice and lots of money. Another may write a book for the purpose of expressing an insight into life, or he may all the time have his eye on markets and sales. He may study art that he may bring more beauty into the world, or his sole idea may be to acquire the skill to do pot boilers. He may seek to be a well-paid shyster or a seeker for justice. In all cases the activities are the same; the outcomes differ. The difference is in the aim.

This was put up to us clearly when the Invisibles took us in charge.

"Your success will depend on your attitude," they told us. "One attitude you may take is the desire to expand the consciousness and understanding for the sake only of the joyous inclusion and comprehension of more and more of the spiritual quality; as one expands one's lungs to breathe deeper of the freshness of the morning. The other attitude – differing so slightly from it that it is even difficult to express the difference clearly – seeks spiritual quality as an ingredient of *personal* spiritual growth. The difference is, as I have said, very subtle; but the one is safe and wholesome; the other is beset with danger, and leads into a confusion unimaginable. The latter seeks primarily *development*, which, when consciously primary as a motive, is a trait of self-centeredness. The other seeks only a capacity for greater inclusion."

The immediate object, they made it equally clear, was a better and more effective technique of living – again for the ultimate purpose of greater usefulness. Nothing, they emphasized, is any good at all unless it is usable in everyday life. If that were not so, there would be no particular object in our being on earth. This is true even of the most abstract and apparently detached strivings and speculations. They must have an umbilical cord to human life or they have no life of their own. The Invisibles called this necessity the principle of "Make-it-so." But, they added as corollary, while actual overt action, visible application and functioning are the usual, inner action and functioning may also be an ingredient of growth. They called this type of action radiation. The emphasis of radiation was one of their objectives.

"A developed person," they explained, "even a developing one, who has come to some recognition of the vital spirit expanding within him, has the opportunity of utilizing that power over the most commonplace episodes of daily life. It is more exactly like water let loose on parched ground than any other figure I can find. Not too great a volume of water at first; but the life-giving spirit of it creeping and seeping, arousing and expanding the paralysis of aridity, everywhere supplying the quickening element that releases the fertility stored in the dusty brown earth. It is just this gentle distribution around you of the spiritual heart force as you feel its expansion within you that will teach you the actuality of spiritual faculties. It is not a directed irrigation like the so-called mental treatment; it is more the rising stream finding its spirit level in opened places among natural encouragements and resistances.

"In other words, the steadiness of the original life-giving impetus is what fosters the best area of growth. Therefore the person who is, who maintains the heart area, the atmosphere, the climate of the spiritual mind – he is the eminent citizen of eternity, the life-educated one, soundly, progressively self-made, permanently cooperative."

— **4** —

There are many methods, as I have said, of consciously cooperating with spiritual forces. And each method has its individual approach, appropriate to itself. Since our own approach was the psychic, most of the early training was largely occupied with the development of the psychic faculties, especially that of communication with the invisible. But here also the means were carefully distinguished from the end. From the very beginning our Invisibles vigorously rejected "psychic power" as an objective.

"The purpose of this exploration," said they, "is not immediately to broaden communication between the obstructed and the unobstructed universes. One of the causes for the instability you note in peoples, individuals, society, thought, is the ultra and sudden ease of communication in time and in space. The radio and the auto are not stabilized. They are too rapid for the assimilation of society in general. Knowing these things probably even better than you, it could not therefore be our purpose to do more at this time than re-establish on the basis of your present knowledge and the demands of your present knowledge – the faith in the divinity of self that is tottering."

This purpose became evident to us after a while, but at the outset it was natural that our first curiosities and wonders should be concerned with the psychic processes themselves. Nevertheless, the Invisibles steadfastly held before us the ultimate objective: that they had for us a "divulgence" – provided they could develop a channel through which to express it.

"It is not," they disclaimed against our uneasiness," a fuzzy, fetishy thing. It's a square-cornered block of facts; and we are going to hurl them right at the world, square and strong. Can't you see what a tough nut that is to crack? Can't you see it's a wedge of spiritual substance, hard-driven into the toughest fiber of the world? It's a good strong blow in an effort to penetrate the – " they hesitated.

"'Hopeless tenuosity of our consciousness,' they say," the Station helped out. "That's funny: we always think of them as tenuous, and here we are just foggy! I don't wonder we can't take hold of anything: and here they are all square-cornered and wedges and things like that, (chuckled) I thought you said we are a tough-fibred world!

"It's a tremendous job because, you see, we are not very intelligent about it. This is a carry-through proposition. They are depending on us for concerted action in planning the demonstration of what is given. That part is for us to manipulate. They plan for it to permeate print and pulpit and pictures and pastimes. (chuckled) I bet you ran out of *p's*."

"It is planned for the moments of relaxation," the Invisible explained, "the most susceptible of moments. Let this thing grow in your collective consciousness, but remember it must be administered popularly. It is like the little thin life-saving line they shoot over to pull over the big one afterwards. It is a small effort now, but it prepares the public mind for the big wedge of demonstration through scientific discovery. Later it will be linked to the slow process of evolution in collective intelligence."

"What the world needs," said they on another

occasion, "is a chemical demonstration of spirituality. You see what the substance of spirituality does to individuals; why not also to the race through standardized education? What an immense breaking down of barriers, if something more than the mere verbal philosophy could be given! If it could be *demonstrated*! Humanity stepping over the line, humanity released from complete physical consciousness. Superstition vanished under education. If the awe of superstition could be lost. Awe is an active agent, both good and evil. Half-education has developed contempt, arrogance, unleashed egotism – banished the awe. Real education must proceed to the point of redeveloping the awe, but enlightened, reinforced. Wipe out the superstition of physical limitations to the human soul. That is where the blow is to fall; the effort to prove.

"Men sickened and died by thousands, 'through the visitation of heaven,' it was piously said, piously believed except by a rebellious few. And the rebellious few strove to wipe out this deep-rooted superstition, just as we are trying to get you to strive now to wipe out the superstition of heaven (i.e., the conventional heaven), which keeps men's souls at best restricted, and at worst sickened by thousands."

— **5** —

As for our own personal share in all this, though the basic Aim was as above set down, the Invisibles might be said to have entertained hopeful intentions rather than an aim. Our job was more in the way of ground breaking than actual construction.

"Push ahead gently," said they. "Each step will be

shown to you. You are getting pictures of our thought, pictures of our life – by that I mean our life *and yours* on the spiritual plane – pictures that will make people think of the spiritual side life in everyday practical terms of living. Your work is twofold. It is a great personal struggle in the line of exploration and treasure seeking; and then the minting of that treasure, when found, into popular coin. You've got to distract attention from the old things of damaged popularity, and establish something bright and shining and lovable, humorous and beautiful, as a balanced ration of life. Before plunging into the tremendous effort necessary to put this over, it is well to cooperate on an objective, understanding clearly the united effort necessary if the purpose is to be achieved."

"So that is it!" commented Betty. "These records are to be the basis. Through them an effort will be made to produce molds of words to contain this in practical form. It will be done painstakingly, bit by bit."

"When this development does come before the world," continued the Invisible, "when it really comes, it will be like a big new invention popped out. And you will have prepared a sort of background for it. What we give you is to be a firmer foundation for people to stand on. The scientific development of this isn't ready yet. It takes time to round out and perfect things. Please note you will not get such scientific explanation as you expect. You will get the reality as we can manage to give it. You can deduce as theory later. We have to work in realities. We mold you to the thing itself. We cannot tell you in words."

"Nevertheless," I pointed out, "words are what we must deal with in conveying ideas."

"That," said the Invisible, "will be your part after the perception is yours. You can reckon on statements as near as we are capable of making them, but only as an accompaniment to the acquisition of the thing itself. Without that, explanations would be sterile. Have patience with our methods; they are more far-seeing in result than you imagine."

My objection that words would be necessary was eventually sustained. But in these early stages there was much discussion among the Invisibles themselves, and some differences of opinion, as to the best procedures.

"At present," urged one school of thought, "it is better not to crystallize it into words which only restrict the conception of it. It can only be comprehended by each person's private practice in spiritual being, in play of heart as it were, unaffectedly following one's intuitive enthusiasms as a healthy animal acquires its experience and coordinations."

"There seems to be somebody impatient for radical departures in other departments of knowledge," said Betty. The argument against it seems to be that it doesn't fit consecutively with what has been given. There's too much of a gap."

"The alternative," said the Invisible, "is to get the reality. After all it has no verbal recording. The first requirement is spiritual development. That is the actual requirement, regardless of whether you can say it or not. If you do not choose it, the material will stay at a dead level, no matter how beautifully it is placed on paper. Personally, of course, you prefer the precise statement."

"I like things that feel," said Betty. "That is why we are successfully adjusted to each other...

"This is a kind of consultation," she went on. "They, each one of them, have a kind of private hope. They're making a balanced ration of it, working together and giving as much of the development as possible at a given time, and interposing as logical a statement of the process as is possible, and dashing off on an occasional tangent as to possibilities ahead transcending our present knowledge of law."

"Great hope is felt," said the Invisible, "that you will understand the necessarily intangible quality of the development – intangible *while in process*. Although the beginnings must be somewhat galling and annoyingly mystic to you, definite results will in time become apparent – a histolysis of creation. If you will kindly keep this in mind it will facilitate the process enormously, especially as the future holds much that is unrecognizable intellectually, or at least unrecorded popularly. The farther afield you go, naturally the more nebulous the beginnings must appear. Do not impose restrictions, intellectual shackles, while the exercise is in progress. Be content to formulate it in one department, master it, possess it, control it, in confidence that you will later translate it.

"The ultimate question before us is how to establish this communication on a common ground of procedure, so that all barriers will be swept away, all arguments and doubts. There is a vast amount of material that has been gathered on this side that would be of the greatest help to you. Heretofore we have not been able to put it to your use except as it has been accepted by you as originating in your own consciousness. In that way a great deal of inspiration is given from this side, but it would be much more valuable if you knew whence it came. You would then open your minds more fully and accept with a certain amount of intelligent gratitude the accumulated treasure of ages."

— **6** —

In the beginning our Invisibles painted a rosy picture of the purpose we were to fulfill. They spared no pains, no urgency, no legitimate spur. This was doubtless necessary to keep us going. But later on they redrew the picture in proper proportions.

"It is perhaps desirable," said they, "in order to maintain the pressure of enthusiasm, to permit at least the beginnings of such work as yours to harbor a hope that is somewhat illusory. On attaining any new state of consciousness, one first of all forgets that it is not necessarily a new thing. One cannot at first gather that others have by multitudes attained the same stage, and even passed beyond it. One feels that one has made a new discovery, and that all that is necessary is to show it to others at once to obtain recognition and acceptance. One dreams of swinging in a body the whole of mankind into the circle of illumination. In the thought one forgets that revelation is merely a measure of development, a yardstick of growth. One forgets that one must attain, not only intellectual conviction, but also emotional conviction: one must attain, not only the satisfied equation, but also the cosmic satisfaction which has nothing to do with the pure mathematics of the intellect. One forgets further that emotional satisfaction of any sort can, by its nature, come only through a personal experience."

There is a lot more to a thing than merely understanding it, they pointed out.

"Intellectual conviction gained through study, through the reading of books, through the experimental examination of evidence, has one function and one function only: it moves the center of interest into the path in which personal experience is most like to be encountered. That is an extremely valuable function. It accelerates what might otherwise be a much delayed recognition, through conscious manifestation, of what is actually prepared.

"The measure of recognition accorded to such statements as may be sent out by book, by demonstration, or by the spoken word, is merely a means of evaluating the degree to which spiritual consciousness has advanced. It is like one drop of a chemical which, by turning to visible color the contents of a vessel, makes evident how much of another chemical is there already in suspension. If a second vessel be so treated, but containing none of the chemical, no effect will be produced. And remember, to continue the figure, if no drop of the first chemical be employed, the color will also lack its visibility. That is at once the limitation and the indispensability of such work as you have been chosen to do on the line of influencing spiritual recognition in a public at large.

"I tell you these things now because you no longer need the stimulus of a false expectation, but are content to rise and fall, cradled on the waves of the universal rhythm of all things. You no longer need a straight line. Straight lines are not beautiful!

"Our object will not be to convince the world of

86

anything except the need for continued conscious spiritual growth. The conviction of one thing or another – or another, will come naturally and easily and inevitably to each individual when he rises by his own specific gravity to that point. It will come to the world generally only when the common consciousness, by its own specific gravity, has also risen to that point."

Thus warned and chastened against undue pride and expectation, we were finally comforted against discouragement.

"Take one step at a time. Say to yourselves: the little group of us here have waked up a little sooner than the rest of them, can see the danger a little clearer, are passionately convinced of the thing to be done. Then we're the ones to do it. It's only the conviction that we are the ones to do it that is going to accomplish it. If you practice that uncomfortable thought a while, you'll get a little action without fussing about it."

"My!" cried Betty. "I feel like the fire department called out, and I don't know where the fire is."

"You see," the Invisible continued, "the trouble is you only halfway realize how we work. That's the trouble. If you work in big passionate directions, the superiority of the force finds its way.

"Please don't say you understand this, because you don't! You don't; you don't; you don't! until you've thought about it no end. It's a lack of passionate direction to life that fails of accomplishment in any direction.

The main thing at present is germinating this thing in yourself; the force behind you at the moment; the fact that it is your business. If that takes complete possession of you, we're off; but until it does we are only planning and waiting for some big thing that may come some day. I tell you the big thing is here. It is an opportunity such as the world has not known for centuries. Each cycle works to a moment of completion and metamorphosis. This is the moment of the coming cycle. The whole health and vitality of that coming cycle depends on the direction of its moment of conception."

VII Contact

TENDER tinted clouds ride from world to world. There is absolution and magic in morning radiance, a hovering secret of eternity.

BETTY

UNTIL there is worship in the heart, a development of intense perception of something vastly superior to the sovereignty of the brain, the recognition of our spiritual sun – until that is actuating, all else is but an intellectual concept.

INVISIBLE

— 1 —

ALL created things are constantly in contact with spiritual forces of some kind. Otherwise they would not exist at all. But for most, even of mankind, this contact is largely automatic and unconscious. We may experience hunches or intuitions or flashes of "inspiration." Generally, however, we do not think of even these as "contact with spiritual forces." They are just obscure workings of our minds, only a little more mysterious than any other of our mental processes.

But when we reach that point of experience which I have described, when we seek to take conscious charge of our own development, a change must come about in this relationship. This is in the nature of things, for taking charge, as we have seen, implies conscious cooperation with spiritual forces. And how can we accomplish that without consciously contacting them?

This, very briefly, is the elementary significance of the term "contact" as used in our records.

Heretofore these pages have dealt with principles that are generally applicable. Therefore they could also be stated in general terms. Now, however, we step over into the particular and the personal, and therefore deal with principles at defy formulation. A man's contact with the spiritual forces is a thing individual to himself. Since men are as unlike as their own thumbprints, it is obvious that the method that works perfectly for me would work illy for you. And that phrasing which gives one man a clear conception will draw blank with another. In dealing with this subject, then, about the only thing we can do is to abandon logical arrangement and set down from the records, almost at random, what was offered us by the Invisibles. The field of selection is the more limited in that the material nearest suited to the personal approach has been used in other books. Much of Betty's first training, it will be remembered, was centered upon contact and the conditions necessary for it. What follows is, with a few repetitions for the sake of a reasonable continuity, some of the material left over.

— 2 —

"When you are conscious of a thing," pointed out an Invisible, "you naturally live in it. When you expand with your heart, or think horizontally, or whatever you want to call it, you've got to come in contact with spiritual substance, for the reason that then you expand beyond your world of senses. You must enter it, if you go beyond your boundaries.

"It is," he acknowledged, "difficult to draw far

enough aside from the countless little deposits in which we live to get into a substance which has not all these subdivisions, but is one flexible vitality. It is not all made up into clothes and houses and bird cages and things. Those concrete things should be wiped out and conditions substituted like enthusiasm, admiration, love – anything that is not made up into articles. That is your real substance, as near as I can get it. You work with them, instead of tools, to create. It is better than knick-knacks, as a substance to live with."

On another occasion:

"Oh my beautiful *aggression* of living!" cried Betty as though in discovery. "That's what it is!"

"It is built entirely of the heart and perceptions," said the Invisible. "The brain is just the steering gear. Listen; it's not a matter of a restless feeling of perpetual motion so much as a feeling of warm existence like quiet but very active rays. It is like the sun growing things."

"This spiritual intelligence, and harmony with law, and contact, and all that collection of words is just one simple natural thing," contributed Betty. "It is a state of health, like a perfection of plant growth or any other vigorous organism, taking in enthusiastically what is bountifully supplied. It is better to look at it that way because 'spiritual contact' sounds a little mystical to some. It is a condition, not an end."

"Holding yourself at this higher pitch is natural," this from the Invisibles. "It is just a matter of pleasurable practice. It is like blending with the sun instead of merely being aware of the sun."

"When I turn to the source of my being," said Betty, "I am as a cell of an harmonious body illuminated beyond my comprehension. My only reaction is one of security and glowing content, a state of rarefied happiness."

"It is," she described on another occasion, "more nearly akin to being aware of a breath-taking and gorgeous Doing and eagerly seeking a minute part in it, allowing the vast Doing itself to flow through and model you to its purposes. You are, however, not passive at all; you are eagerly active, as a child is active."

And here is another which has already been printed, but which cannot be omitted if we are even to attempt an adequate glimpse. It is Betty speaking.

"Supposing," said she, "you had always been of the general buoyancy of a flatiron, and suddenly someone showed you how, by continuously opening yourself up, you became more like a balloon. Very little difference, you see, between you and the air. You are simply an envelope for it, taking the certain amount of it which differentiates you. Now substitute for that substance contained inside the balloon – which also supports it outside – the universal vital quality of life. You feel it everywhere, in the woods and the waters, the endless manifestations of vitality, pulsing and vibrating in contrast to the inanimate things we handle so constantly. Get that first conception of life, life, life. Try to see what life is, try to grasp it, compare it in every way you know. It takes a long, long time of training yourself just merely to *conceive* of that life power, what it actually seems like in essence, and not merely in its varied forms. Then by degrees, if you can associate yourself enough with it consciously to rest in it, depend upon it, then the great secret of these teachings is yours. The rest is the power of appropriation; how strong and free you can become partaking of it, and how rhythmically you can partake of its cyclic movement."

"Feels sort of like a blind person walking along," was her attempt on another occasion, "I feet when I get in a sunspot of power, and I try to keep in it, and when I stray out of it I try to get back. I know it's there, and I just have to make my senses so acute that I can keep in it or get back to it if I stray. Each person must play his own mental game in this thing."

"It is not" – this is from an Invisible – "a reaching for anything; it is absolutely the contrary. It is a secure embryonic stirring, happily stretching into one's own particular universe, basking in growth sensations, until one establishes one's self in permanent strength from the center of the heart of life, acquiring very gradually and sustainedly the consciousness of the similar process going on in every living thing. This gives inward significance and the possession of inward companionship with the spiritual nature of that and all other particularized manifestations of universal life. Never allow strain or any affectation of mind to enter into the practice of one's individual heart expansion or spiritual flame feeding. Let the flame lick up life as it instinctively will, remembering that it spreads its radiations as one recognizes and feeds it properly."

And another time:

"Willingness to receive is alone not sufficient to

establish contact," the Invisible pointed out. "The mere willingness is not motivating; in fact, it has a great difficulty to be overcome in what might be called a *suctional* quality, a greed without the contribution of the ardor of soul which maintains the higher intelligence without depletion in its own degree. The mere willingness to receive, or what we have called the suctional state of mind, *precipitates* the force above it; *reduces* it to a lower manifestation, in which it no longer functions as a quickening inspirational force. It becomes an intellectual 'record,' not a gift of growth silently available through you to others of your degree."

Again Betty contributes her own individual definitions.

"I ease my body into pleasant memories. I lull it to comfort. I think of the wind in the pines; or feel the sun's warmth – perfect physical peace and enjoyment; entirely concerned with my own body. Life surrounding me is nonexistent. I know that each side of my spinal column, placed in comfort, lie strong, life-sustaining muscles. I will retire all my strength and consciousness into that fastness. It is as if a trap door were closed. I am within myself: content.

"Slowly, in that content, there forms an interest, a desire to expand. I do not define any more: I feel. I feel that there is a secret exit; something awaiting exploration; something highly desirable and exciting. It lies in a different direction from that by which I entered, and closed. On one side I can dissolve all separateness. Something can flow into me, and I can flow out to it with the same comfort with which I relaxed the body; only within the comfort is desire and latent strength, release into a well-being which I cannot define in words. It is an essence of life, not to be put down in lesser terms. Roughly and poorly I have attempted to define the word contact."

"Can you," said the Invisible, attempting a definition of the sensation, "make yourself conscious for a moment of nothing but the blood which flows through your veins? It's life, life, life, life! Now hold that idea as often as you can. It is the great permanent sensation of existence, whether you express it through your body, or I express it this moment through my body, or on and on indefinitely. It is the *control* of this sensation that makes you a master in equilibrium, able to cooperate, we will say; for it is not control exactly, nor manipulation, but cooperation with all other forms through which the vitality passes. However, this may be acknowledged in various philosophic or scientific forms, it's the imaginative *use* of it, the actual physical effect it has on your body and whole combined make-up that people don't realize.

"It is savoring your oxygen," he groped further. "It is like bolting your food if you just Lo on breathing without any particular feeling that each breath is a great kinship. You can take *celestial* breaths. That savors your oxygen."

"It is," contributed Betty, "the instant of its passing through you that is your moment of divinity, absolute unity. Thus individual life is fed. Everything I get is the sum of these moments of unity."

Never mind whether you understand fully or not.

"There are," observed Betty apropos of this, "so

many things in this kind of companionship that are delicious; so many things I share, participate in without understanding. Something like being a dog. His associations with his higher beings are very satisfactory and intensely desirable, but he doesn't altogether comprehend them. He just enjoys them."

Nevertheless, though we may not "altogether comprehend," there is no reason at all why we should not become fully aware. Plenty of things exist in our environment, impalpable and unknown, which need only intelligent action on our part to become visible. Radio, for a simple example. The room is full of it, but we are unaffected until we take measures to bring it to audibility.

"How do you set about trapping radio waves?" challenged the Invisible. "A human being can be, according to his own desire, unaware of life forces passing through him, in which he is immersed, but he can also voluntarily incorporate himself with them. In order to do this, some faint idea of process, some symbol helping in the adjustment, must be given for those who are starting from this particular angle.

"Supposing you localize a region of the body to become an awareness-mechanism, a receiving station, a sensitized hospitable region where life force is welcomed and acknowledged, we'll say. You know it is all around you, but you've got to admit it to yourself somehow. So you take the poetic region of the heart. Without intellectual effort or reason you childlikely center your perceptive faculties, all the emotional warmth of which you are capable, in this open channel of the heart. You must have some symbol of entrance into the physical being in order to work in these new terms, to comprehend these especial laws.

"Now this is a great life force, undifferentiated or intentioned or specialized. It is as if one strung one's self, like a bead, through an aperture of the heart, on this great life chain connected with all other created beings.

"Now if you will follow this simplest exposition of law in truly childlike fashion, step by step, you will actually create for yourself the sensation of the entrance into your being of the universal creative life force. Let it continually flow through you, and as often as possible clear moments in your life to circulate it through your being, stimulating mind and body and every part. Nourished by it, let your mental faculties plan its utilization.

"This can be successful only after deep and powerful realization of the sensation of the great spiritual blood stream. Here comes the almost insurmountable difficulty of translation. The sensation of being in this spiritual blood stream pouring on earth conditions is not to be contained in words. I long intensely to work out for you some concept of the spiritual blood stream. It has always been inadequately screened by the word God."[*]

---

[*] It may help formulation if the reader will also look up in *The Betty Book*, pages 40-43; 46; 48-49; 52-53; 180-181. Also *Across the Unknown*, Chapter XI; pages 59-60; 188-192. And finally *The Road I Know*, pages 182-187; 192-193; 202-205.

— 3 —

Many hints were given as to the use of contact in our days and hours. The best of these have been presented in the other books, but a few should be quoted here for completeness.

"The first business of each day," said the Invisibles, "is a recognition of the sun of your life: unquestioning and eager heart-lifting acknowledgment of the warm, loving, positive creative force of the universe beyond our knowledge. Always give time to purify and clothe fittingly your spirit to contemplate the unknown great Causal Force operating through each living thing. Unless you make a conscious exercise of this, conscious power is not yours throughout the day. Use your analytical faculties to sense just how matter-of-fact and ardent and unquestioning is your acceptance and expectancy of this association. It comes to you; it operates in the minutiae of your affairs; your only concern is to convince yourself of it. It should be the one thing you are completely, absolutely sure of, and trust in face of all obscurations. The living belief is your part. The more established and ardent the conviction, the greater your caliber.

"At intervals during the day, stop for a moment and rate the percentages of attention and ardor you are preparing to put into your various affairs. Examine these percentages as if they were allotments of finances in a business budget. Then step aside from them a moment, return to the concept of your business of eternal purposes, and compare the two. Which ones of your ordinary activities can you vitalize to the point where they help you unite with other lives in greater inclusion of the consciousness which we are striving to make for you an everyday affair?

"Again we are attacking the interpenetration of spiritual force with earth inertia. In time its importance will be so evident you will wonder you could have endured the chill of self-containment. Once you get the *feel* of it, the pleasure of its warm expansiveness will be sufficient pursuit in itself."

"Where," wondered Betty, "did all the dullness and apathy of the world come from? How did it accumulate? How did we cut ourselves off? How did we become so spiritually paralyzed? Where in our history did we stop acknowledging the inflowing creative substance of us and think we could accomplish in living apart from conscious acknowledgment of it? We cut off the flow to our souls, and try to force it into such strange channels! "

Another time she herself attempted a restatement of the process.

"It is a simple technique. The very first thing always is the tuning of yourself, your leap or levitation of heart to your Source – the absolute tuning of yourself. You are then imbedded in something so much more potent than yourself, so incomprehensibly secure, that all you can do is to sense the comfort, lend yourself rapturously to it.

"Next, while you are completely comfortable, composed and warmed and reassured of your divinity – while you are there, before any tensions can Stan, while power is upon you – decide what you are going to do when you are farther away from it; when you have changed your focus. Then proceed wholeheartedly to use your ordinary faculties in clean-cut application to the thing in hand.

"What I am trying to say is: don't mix up your regions of consciousness. When occupied with something practical, don't keep wondering if you are working in a spiritual way. The Source will not desert you until you lose your surety and strangle yourself with tensions. Then you cut it off; you chill yourself.

"The important thing is the sensing how long you can work masterfully without renewing yourself. Each person must decide for himself when he is depleted and recharge himself for mastery. It is your individual rhythm that determines this. There is nothing difficult about it. Just do not go on working when you feel that depreciation has set in. Then a momentary return to attunement is all that is necessary; *provided* you have made a strong and accustomed home of it. But while working in our present limited earth consciousness, it is best to be clean-cut in wholehearted application to the thing in hand. It is not necessary to be continually hurrying back to reassure yourself of the spiritual quality. It will not desert you until you yourself deliberately shut it out.

"The two outstanding points are: to spend always plenty of time tuning yourself in comfort at your Source; plenty of time to have it well established; and then never to doubt that it follows you when your *mind* is completely freed from it in the minutiae of work."

VIII Measure for Measure

AS SOON as you begin to live in the truth that you hold all power within you, new worlds will open up in A directions like magic.

INVISIBLE

— 1 —

THE first great laws in human functioning we have dealt with as The Law of Overflow and The Law of the Positive Ingredient. They are interdependent. We found that we obtained the dynamics of our forward evolution from the Positive Ingredient, whose great reservoir is the Invisible World; and that it is perfectly possible to make conscious contact with that reservoir.

But now we encounter a third great law, and this we may call The Law of Complement. It, too, can be simply stated.

'Help can come to us from the Invisible, but only in Complement to our own effort.'

— 2 —

It is difficult to grasp the full implication of this statement. Or at least we ourselves were slow in getting to it. The Invisibles told it to us often enough, and in a sufficient variety of forms. We took their urgings to "make the dead lift," to "make it so," to work hard if we expected them, the Invisibles, to do anything for us, only as spurs to action. The implication to us was that the Invisibles would give or withhold their help according as we were good and deserving children. It did not dawn on us that the giving or withholding was not in their choice. Yet time after time they plainly said so, in so many words. Here is how some of it reads, as it came to us scattered over the years.

"We are not permitted to carry the growth itself. That is in your hands."

"The force we bring into the world comes from a combination of conditions created by the person himself. We can only take advantage of that combination. Once a person of his own force establishes it, we can act on it. The initial step is your work. This force is, roughly speaking, emanations from you which meet complementary forces from this side."

"The energy with which you demand of us will be the measure of what you will get. *It is not so much the energy of demand as the showing of a force that calls its complement.* It is the energy of measure for measure, given and received."

And many more, similar, that pointed so exactly to what was meant that I now marvel how I was so stupid as to miss it. Some of the references were not so direct but were still sufficiently pertinent. Talking specifically of raising vibration, the Invisible said:

"It is best to remind you that this control, this acquisition of raised vibration – whatever you choose to call it – is absolutely within the desire of the individual.

It is a thing one builds or does not build, according to his caliber. There is no use craving what you do not put out the energy to take."

What misled us was the fact that we were then being given the technique, so we confined the application of what was being said to that particular job.

"There is," said the Invisible, "a curious reciprocity about this. We can only take advantage of effort, and you have to supply the effort. You happen to be at a friend's house tipping a table. There is our chance. But we might shout at you ten years.

"We cannot do your end of it. Make a start, no matter how gropingly or blunderingly. The initiative of your objective efforts is vitally necessary for the complement of our directive efforts. We cannot direct *nothing*.

"Let us call it inspirational force for the sake of giving it a name. It comes from a *combination of conditions, created by the person himself*. We only take advantage of the condition. It is very difficult to do much toward creating that condition. Once a person of his own force establishes it, we can act on it. The initial step is your work. We gather naturally around those who permit us to. It is something like digging a well to earth, only we work with peculiar forces of attraction. We hesitate to use words like soul yearnings, for instance, because in your mind they have other significances from ours. The idea is that we cannot in any satisfactory degree work on an unreceptive person.

"By that brute force you accomplish the first dead

lift. It is just determination and faith that helps that first sheer lift. That manifestation with yourself you must get before you get any response. That is what people do not realize. They don't put any strength into it, and when it won't work at once, they go the other way. You must get the strength yourself."

But, had we noticed it, the same principle was many times applied to other of our activities than the mere technique of the teaching. For instance, one day inspiration was the subject under consideration.

"Inspiration," said they, "is purely a complementary force. That means that it is only placed as a decorative capital on a column you have already built. That is absolutely so. Inspiration comes only in attraction to some definite output, some definite production. It cannot come unless it has a container. Inspiration fills only what is prepared for it. It is like electricity, it has to be brought into a mechanism made ready for it.

"Your progress is in your own hands. We can do little but watch you gain necessary strength before we can help you further. *That is the law. We can act only as the complement to the act.*"

— **3** —

Now in that last statement is one word on which the real understanding of the law of complement depends. It is the word can.

Note what the Invisible says: "We can act only as the complement to the act." Not "we will act" or "we shall act." "We can act." "That is the law." The phrasing means exactly what it says. What we loosely call the spiritual forces are *unable*, under the law, to act directly on the obstructed universe. They must have something to complement, something to spark them, to set them in motion.

So when we fail to get the response, or the help, or the communion we desire, either from the Invisibles or the higher spiritual forces, the refusal is not whim, or an arbitrary judgment of our deserts. And yet at times it seems just that. The Invisibles are able to help us, for again and again they have done so, at times almost "miraculously" it seems. But at other times, in predicaments when it would seem that the most misanthropic would in sheer charity lend a hand, they pay us no attention at all. There is no sense to it – if they are indeed our friends and wish us well. We do not like to think them that kind of people.

However, if we accept this Law as binding, we can understand. The Invisibles are always there, always ready. But they can act only when we ourselves offer something strong and worthy of complement. They are ever eager to give and to help, but they are constrained by the law to "measure for measure, given and received."

— **4** —

Like all general laws, this one acts universally, depending for its effects on the medium in which it operates. It explains many things. For instance, the usual experience of "sitters for communication" or psychic phenomena. Sometimes they get good results, sometimes very poor results, sometimes utterly misleading results, or none at all. They use great ingenuity in explaining these discrepancies. Some times the explanations become almost fantastic. As a matter of fact, under this law of complement, a "good" sitting results when the sitters have enough sincerity, honesty and, above all, selfless purpose or aim to bring to the séance sufficient material for the Invisible operators to work with. A "poor" sitting is of course the reverse. And when, as often happens, the Invisibles terminate any session of any kind with the statement that "power wanes" or "the juice is giving out," that does not mean, though we usually interpret it so, that they, the Invisibles, have come to the meeting on a certain tankful of gas, but rather that we, the sitters, have come to the end of our contribution for the occasion.

The same principle carries into the more spiritual content of prayer. The subject will be later treated, but it is enough to say that if we get response it must be in supplement to that which we offer from our hearts. And without that offering there shall be only silence.

A wider application is evident in the processes of evolution. If human consciousness itself, mankind as a whole, gets its power to advance only in complement to its own constructive contribution, then we can understand why the first stages of evolution were so slow, and why at present the pace accelerates. Primeval conditions were torpid. Primeval man had a pretty meager equipment of either insight or what we call the moral forces. He was, perforce, immersed in the seething egoism necessary for mere survival. He had not the slightest idea of benefiting anybody but himself. His purpose was to save his skin or make his leisure and comfort. Only occasionally, but neither largely nor often, did self-interest extend into wider construction. The aggregate positive contribution of the whole earth make-up, physical and human, was very slight. Evolution had to do the best it could in complement. With this scant seeding to plant and reap and plant again, how could progress be anything but slow? But in the long sequence of harvests, each more abundant than the last, is it not evident why in the latter days of our evolution in consciousness we seem to be fairly bursting forth into the clear of understanding – though we have still a long way to go!

For the first time the process is groping its way out of the automatic. In all ages a few of the illuminated have understood what it is all about, but they have been so very few that we have set them in a class apart – saints, holy men, saviors. Now men as a race are fairly on the verge of taking conscious and personal charge. In the not-too-remote future no longer will they act only from that native instinct for creative inventive building which distinguishes mankind from the purely instinctive animal. Nor will the motive be preponderantly self-interest. Then, it is reasonable to infer, as the opportunity for complement is more abundantly offered, the pace of evolution will correspondingly hasten.

— 5 —

Fortunately the automatic has a wider meaning, or we might still be back with the cave men. As, for instance, what an Invisible pointed out to us in the course of a talk an esthetics.

"Each honest and vital effort, whether conscious or unconscious, toward beauty or that overflow that makes for beauty, is a constructive power. And the sum total of those efforts, whether in a humble crocheted

107

lamp mat, or in an attempt at stage effects in the theatre, or in an honest though pathetic attempt at decorating a hotel lobby, or a flower over the flower girl's ear – all make in the aggregate a formidable onward-pushing construction which, even though scattered and comparatively unmarked, goes far to overbalance the spectacular, disheartening destructions that get in the newspaper headlines and worry everybody with the idea that the country is going to the dogs. It's the aggregate. The Recording Angel idea is not far off – with his debits and credits."

Nor, the Invisible rather ironically observed, need we too seriously indulge our egoistic complex that we are, as the saying goes, the only pebbles on the beach. Evolution could get along without us! In the larger view of evolution as a whole we must not overlook the fact that the very processes of nature, as far as they are harmonious, add their quota to that which may be complemented.

There is no occasion, the Invisible underscored this point, to deny its spiritual complement to the bird song at dawn, or the smooth, exact, beautiful interplay of the natural forces that keep the rhythm of the tides or the rains. Possibly, in the very torpid beginnings of evolution, that may have been the only tiny power that, by ever so little, tipped the wheel off center! Volitional action had its innings only eons later! Certainly man's consciousness was not then involved: man was not there.

In a manner of speaking he is still "not there." But he is getting there, and like all other evolution the pace is accelerating. One further step and he will have arrived at least at the point of taking charge consciously. He must come fully to realize that, by this law, each act of his life, no matter how trivial, does offer a force to meet its complement. He already appreciates that action has consequence in the physical world, and therefore he puts thought and will into his efforts. Only now is he beginning dimly to sense that there are also other effects, in the invisible or spiritual. When he does so fully, he will direct just as much conscious thought to bringing about these effects as he does to the obvious of the physical. He will realize that in planting a seed, or tightening a nut on the assembly line, raking up the leaves, or washing the dishes, he is not only producing a flower or a part of a motor car or a tidy household, but he is offering a chance for spiritual complement. The satisfaction he gets from the material accomplishment must thereby be enhanced. And the sense of drudgery must dissolve in the perception that what he must do releases the possibility of a higher accomplishment.

No matter what our estate, great or small, or how straightly we seem to be bound by triviality, if consciously we realize – give thought – that here in our hands is the choice, to offer or to withhold a chance for particularization and complement of that which comes from the Source, then will the occasion overflow.

So there is the act, and the realization we put into it. The latter is what gives it its ultimate value; not the mere external result. Therefrom comes our sense of its importance, and its meaning and pleasure and satisfaction. If we have to the full that feeling of *contribution*, we shall savor one of the greater meanings of the words in the Bible:

"Ask and it shall be given you; seek and ye shall

find; knock and it shall be opened to you."

But note that you must *ask, seek, knock* before you will be given or will find or have it opened. They are the complements to your own act – and impossible without it.

IX Meditation

NEVER reach out for this world with concentration of mind, but with what I might call inflation of spirit.

INVISIBLE

— 1 —

CONTACT, as I have said, is a matter of individual experience and definition. It is hoped that the books and the previous pages have at least given the reader a basis for his own impression. It does not matter how diverse – and divergent – these impressions may be. Their value is in picturing to each an objective in which he can have faith. Now it is possible to be less vague. Granted an objective, how are we to go about reaching it? How are we to achieve this Contact?

For this purpose there are really two positive exercises, so to speak. Or perhaps it would be better to say two aspects of the same exercise. We name them meditation and prayer. These are so much alike that to the inexperienced they might appear to be one and the same. Nevertheless there is a useful distinction.

Meditation might be defined as a consciously entered state of attunement with the Source of all being; a conscious, purposeful offering of ourselves as a channel for the flow-through from the Source; and finally, a conscious directing or *intentioning* of the flow toward some desirable purpose.* Its nature is essentially active, autonomous.

Prayer as a state of consciousness is also an attunement, but rather in the purpose of communion with, or submission to, a Higher Power than of overt activity. Its action is more passive and receptive. Except for these slight distinctions the terms meditation and prayer can be considered, for practical purposes, as nearly enough synonymous.†

As to a technique of meditation we received quite a volume of exact directions. I say a technique, for this method might not be adapted to everyone alike. Nevertheless it is worth presentation, somewhat condensed, if only for the reason that any kind of blueprint in these matters is almost unique in its precision.

"This series of exercises I want you to do," began the Invisible, without preliminary.

"1. Lie down on the floor, comfortable, relaxed; the way a dog does. Then imagine yourself above your body; imagine yourself as a bird flying; or an airplane flying; or yourself in an a lane.

---

* The details of this subject are so thoroughly discussed in *Anchors to Windward*, pages 108-132, that they need not be repeated here.

† They, too, have been elsewhere discussed more in detail. See *The Betty Book*, Chapter XVI; *Anchors to Windward*, Chapter XVI; and references under Prayer in the index of *The Stars Are Still There*.

"2. Then think of a river in connection with the blood stream in your body; as flowing all through; a constant vital flow easily but securely, as water falls down hill, not fast, but in the rhythm of a river.

"3. Think of beautiful groves of fruit, vineyards, the coming harvest of which you are to partake that is going to build up the channel through which the river is to flow – the body.

"4. Think of the air as something delicious and sweet, as something you want very much. You are to take the air consciously in your lungs. Think of it as full of life, as the sunshine is full of life.

"5. Think of your body as a piece of machinery that you must operate and take care of, keep oiled and clean, like that of your boat or car. You must consciously – remembering the first exercise – try to feel the flow of the blood, the ease of the machinery.

"6. Think that God created man in His own image; that you are God, a part of the great Whole which creates itself, and which is going to help you recreate its own machinery."

Those were the simple rules laid down for one just starting his first formal meditation periods. Of course the ultimate "nice intermingling," as Betty called it, is something grown into by much more inclusive techniques, but here is one way to begin. We soon could see and acknowledge the unwisdom of telling exactly what to expect from continued meditation. Such detail was much too likely to substitute anticipation for simply doing the present job. And also there would be temptation to kid one's self into the idea that the result described has been reached long before such is the fact. The value is in the process without reference to results.

Referring to Exercise No. 1, in the above schedule, the Invisible gave these further hints. You are not to "make your mind blank," said he; that is impossible.

"In the first exercise you not only rise above your body; but also above your brain-mind. You do not empty out extraneous thoughts from the latter: you leave them there, just as you leave your body there. You do not live down among them, following them about; any more than you live down among your body sensations, following them about. Ordinarily when a spider gets on your body, for instance, your whole attention rushes to the spot. But when you are absorbed in some interest – or are asleep – you detach just enough of your mind to remove it, "mechanically," you say. So with impingements on the brain-mind, either by stray or extraneous thoughts, or by small bodily sensations that demand some measure of adjustment. Thus they do not force you to abandon your present purposes.

"It is easier to avoid being diverted from these exercises by the tendency of the conscious mind to lure you down its own free associations, if you remember that the conscious mind is a creature of time. Left to itself, it tends to deal with the past – what you have done, memory; or with the future – what you are going to do; speculation. It but rarely, and then only in intensive concentration on something specific, stops exclusively in the exact present. Refuse to budge from the moment of Now. Let the conscious mind escape you to the right hand or the left – the past or the future – if it will, but do not accompany it. Thus the you-yourself can poise in its necessary elevation above the body, above the brain-mind, in the superconscious that touches the fringe of the timelessness of a Now that contains all the rest. This statement has little value or meaning as a mere statement, but has great value as a hand-up to actual experience.

"When you have realized this as an experience, you can train the conscious mind not to pluck at you unreasonably and unmannerly and improperly. "

Obviously this is a single and simple exercise of the imaginative principle, designed to shift the balance of attention. To some the foregoing directions will suffice, but the Invisibles had a further refinement to focus upon if capturing the sensation proved difficult.

"After rising above your body in general, until that has become more or less automatic, concentrate on rising above your HEAD. As soon as you have the impression that the breath through your nostrils is below (in space) your mind, instead of above it, you will have gained this.

"The mental attitude at present," they further suggested, "is of observation, not of doing. You are using imagination, but it is not the imagination of the brain-mind; it is imagination of the body. The imagination of the body, as distinguished from the imagination of the mind, is that it is imagination of construction *through sensation*. That of the mind is imagination of construction *through idea*."

So much for Exercise No. I, the getting away from awareness of the body. As for Exercise No. 2, the consciousness of flow-through, the Invisible warned against strain and self-consciousness.

"You do not *think* the process of the vital flow by any applied effort of the imaginative will. You simply *note the fact*. The fact is facilitated by your attention, but is not inaugurated by it."

Or, putting it in another way:

"When you think of the vital flow in your body *you* not *initiating* anything. This stream is already flow; through your body. If it did not, you would not be alive at all. You are coming into observation of an already existent and continuous fact."

Once we recognize the sensation, they continued the instruction, we should try consciously to establish it as a condition that is to continue throughout the twenty-four hours, or until the next meditation period. We instruct it to "go on working." "Then," said they, "we must pause deliberately from time to time and for a second or two take notice that it still is going on. That does not mean an effort to 'recapture' the feel of the flow-through, but to bring to awareness that it is going on. The final step is to be able to give full attention as usual to all the necessities and details of daily life and work, and *still* to remain aware – *all the time* – *underneath* those activities – of the feel of the flow. A sort of double attention, as it were, but without diminishing either attention. This may be facilitated by deliberate practice during meditation. Select some small topic of daily life and think about it, but see if you can do so and still keep full awareness and encouragement of the process of inducing the flow-through."

It is well not to tackle this "double attention" experiment too soon.

That is all we are supposed to do, as beginners in technique. But ultimately, the Invisibles pointed out, as an anticipatory parenthesis, the job will be to develop better conditions in ourselves for the flow.

"What you are creating is the channel for the flow. The strength of the flow is automatically determined by the strength of the channel. Your building is to strengthen the channel in order to permit, to deserve, so to speak, a more vital flow."

For the purpose of this building we must next attend to the gathering of the materials therefore, which is the real significance back of the very imaginative third and fourth exercises. Later, from her vantage of the unobstructed, Betty impressed on us that she now works in essences; and that, in a way, is exactly what we are called upon to do here. From the "beautiful groves of fruit, vineyards, the coming harvest," and all the rest of which we are advised to think, what we really draw is the essence of abundance, vitality, life which they embody, a distillation of those qualities. We are not sufficiently advanced, as yet, effectively to take the pure thing, from the source itself, so we must allow ourselves – in meditation – to be drawn in thought to that imaginative image which most nearly expresses the particular "abundance" we most need.

"The sense-of-abundance exercise," said the

Invisible, "is to be done as though you are feeding into the stream the necessary ingredients for aliment and construction from an abundance at your disposal and in which you dwell."

There is no profit in specific examples. Each will find his own symbol according to the shape of his head. But, said the Invisible, "it should be noted that there are two sorts of abundance to be taken in – that of *force* or power for construction, and that of material of which the construction may be built. Simple examples of the two are the sun and, the field of grain. The sun is abundance in its purest form. It is the origin and source of all the physical abundances. "But," warned the Invisible, "it is too pure an essence for sole diet. It must be transformed into variation – as it is transformed into the plants and animals and minerals which make up the expression of the life force."

A more assimilable image to conjure up for the pure force side of the intake, they suggested, might be a waterfall.

"It is a force of abundance compounded of many sorts of forces. Its plunge is the combination of the force that lifted the vapor from the sea, the various forces that made the winds to move, the air to cool, the vapor to condense, the resultant stream to flow downhill, until at the brink of the plunge is a great and mighty and resistless abundance of actual power that may be breathed in as a single thing, an element of refreshment and vitality. This is a good example of what we meant by a *distillation* of abundance. It is thus prepared for ingestion, as the varied elements comprised in physical food are concentrated by natural processes in the grain of wheat."

Whatever the "distillation" from whatever imagined objects or conditions, we must not, in this earlier meditation, try to direct the force to any specific purpose of our own. Right now we are merely attracting the material for construction, for growth.

"You dump it into the vital stream you have thought of as flowing through you in the second exercise. You do not think of using it in any, specific way. That use is an automatic process of your mechanics of life. It is analogous to the use made of the denser material you put at the disposal of your bodily processes by the ingestion of food. You supply the food: the automatic mechanics of your life processes distribute its uses. Neither the physical nor the spiritual uses are as yet your conscious affair. This distillation is as material as food, but in the subtler realm of the Beta body. It is not a mere idea.

"In the world of abundance, of which you think imaginatively, and from which you draw the constructive aliment, the distillation is various, and not homogeneous. The aliment should not be a mere hash or soup of everything. Your diet should be various and discriminating. It is like your physical diet, selective. We showed you, in shallow and ripple and crossing and pool, one of your Alaska rivers; and you were a bit impatient with yourself because you thought your 'mind was wandering.' But that, for the moment, and as a specific example, was a specific distillation of a specific form of abundance, which at that time you were ingesting by means of the breathing-in symbol. It would, however, be a mistake to will your imagination toward any specific form of abundance. Your attention must be permitted to saunter. It will then be attracted toward the need of the moment. There is a distinction, however, between this and idle wandering, which can be understood only through the actual experience: a certain basic alertness of spiritual appetite. The breathing-in is merely a connecting symbol through which you approach a contact. The contact is determined by your spiritual instinct, and not through your intellectual interests or appraisements."

It is not now our job – it must be emphasized – to insist on the exact application of whatever force we are inducing. "Holding the thought" for the purpose of "demonstrating" a mink coat or a new situation or what we think to be wise in the way of specific aid is out. That will come later, if at all, when we do become wise.

"The specific utilization of the balanced ration in the construction of your channel is not your affair; any more than is the varied use of the constituents of your blood stream in the construction of your body. Only the judicious and intelligent direction of your diet. Nor is it your business to attempt with the brain-mind to emphasize either the force aspect or the material aspects of its constituents; nor to strive, with whatever good intentions, to influence construction toward the 'more spiritual,' or the 'more materially robust.' That is equivalent to reanalyzing ingested food. Accept results happily and unsearchingly. Their quality is appropriate to your own, and dependent on it. Your quality is your stature, to which you cannot add merely by taking thought. Distinguish between growth and construction."

And on another occasion, and by another Invisible:

"The main thing to watch is the intrusion unbeknownst of small desires. You must brush from the integrity of this meditation all trace of personal inclinations." Not that arriving at decision in the specific instance may not happen through meditation; but it will be, in that case, without the conscious use of the intellect. The problem may be formulated; set on the back of the stove, so to speak, and dismissed from the mind.

And, finally, there should be no strain in the attention to intake.

"When," said the Invisible, "you have imaginatively pictured any one of these numerous abundances, so that you have come to the visualization of breathing in its distillation, then it is not necessary, during that period, to continue to hold it continuously and persistently in mind. The channel is connected, and the flow-in will continue in that period of doing the exercise."

— **3** —

These exercises, and others which may occur to us as practical, should be concentrated upon one at a time until their control is effected. But whatever their number, they are really integral.

"They are of course," said the Invisible, "actually one thing; or, rather, by means of them you attain to one thing. Eventually they blend together, so that if you touch any one of them, enter by any one of them, the others are automatically entered also. Any one implies all the others.

"So," the Invisible followed out the logic of this, "the next step after acquiring a fair facility at these exercises, is to try to discard the imaginative symbols and to enter directly into the pure *sensation*. Thus in the first exercise forget the *idea* of the airplane, or the bird, or whatever device you have used to get the *idea* of rising above your body. Forget the *idea* of being above your body. See if you cannot enter directly the *sensation* you experience when you have succeeded in doing so. Confine yourself to the first exercise until you have caught the knack."

When these two things have been grown into the direct entrance into the essence, the sensation of whatever symbols have been useful; and the blending of all the separate components into one direct action – then we are ready for the next step forward.

"That accomplishment," said the Invisible, "comes only with practice of each separately, and in their due order. Like a golf swing. You cannot think of them all at once; you can think of but one thing at a time. But you can, ultimately, enter the benefit of their blend, when practice has synthesized them into a state of being that functions – like any being – as a whole.

"The establishment of this state of being, as a whole thing, is best made consciously at the beginning of the day. It is best entered by the door of the abundances. You will allow your sauntering instinct to select its day's ration through the imaginative contemplation – which is also appropriation – of the form of abundance, both of force and material, which attracts its appetite. This abundance is then there present for the day's needs. On it you will draw for sustenance and refreshment momentarily, from time to time, without necessity of the elaborate devices of specific 'exercises.' You will do so by the simple device

122

of rising to it, bringing with you for its automatic utilization the orderly and interdependent mechanisms which the exercises have constructed, controlled and operated by the orderly subconscious you have trained."

— 4 —

"I have a great plea to make," said the Invisible; "I want you to come with me, all of you who are ready. There is only one way to do it. Part of your time, when you are not at your work, I want you to lay aside all effort at understanding and interpretation, and come out into the wide outside and bask. Just say to yourselves: 'I will lay aside the symbols for the reality. I will be a mere responsive plant to unwordable influences. My busy, near-sighted little self is quieted, set aside for the purpose of expanding a great and dormant power within me. It is weak; it barely records impressions as yet; but through it surges all that is enduring.'

"You must periodically withdraw yourself from your work and your world, if you would keep your vitality in it. It's a great secret law that must be obeyed if you would give forth life and create. Don't wither your good growth; take the sustenance it needs to preserve the spirit through its lower forms of manifestation. The spirit is vast outside. Think always of your work as the mere letting of the sun through windows. Do not use up the atmosphere in the rooms of your mind. Keep firmly in mind the hygiene of the spirit.. It is absolutely necessary for its persistence in deteriorating surroundings. What you are doing looms large in importance, but always be possessed and directed by the conviction that it is a mere crystallization of an underlying spiritual reality. This reality must be continually associated with for refreshment. Therefore bask in it as it suits your temperaments."

X Prayer

TELL him every time he is tempted to light his little fire in order to see better in the dark places, to lie down and rest. The sun will give you better light.

INVISIBLE

— 1 —

THERE is a slight distinction, as we have seen, between the terms prayer and meditation. Meditation can well take the direction of prayer; and prayer, in turn, from one point of view, is the highest form of meditation. One thing they have in common: the induction of conscious contact with our Source. The main difference is that meditation is for the purpose of directed intake and use, and prayer for the purpose of a more *acquiescent* communion. That is a rough distinction, but sufficient for present purposes.

The point was brought up by a question.

"Is prayer," asked one of us, "simply a mechanical means of getting in touch with a source of assistance, or is it essentially a realization process?"

"If you mean the formal thing called prayer," replied the Invisible, "its value is solely that it implies a certain effort and desire to come into contact with what you differentiate as spiritual forces. If you mean the actual feeling of communion or harmony or mystic contact which many people describe as the *state of prayer*, it is a realization.

"It is a realization – but do not minimize the sincere formal prayer, because that sort of effort and desire is necessary from your end, before what we have called our end can operate."

"A formal prayer may also be a state of prayer?"

"A formal prayer may very successfully INDUCE a state of prayer," amended the Invisible, "but it is not the words of the formal prayer that bring realization. It is only that the words form an easy route."

"It is not necessary that what you call a formal prayer be stated in words, is it?"

"It is an effort and a desire," said the Invisible.

Prayer, then, is essentially a communion. But also it has certain results, certain definite by-products. One of these is a uniquely peaceful and harmonious state of mind. And this, in turn, makes for clarity of insight.

"Don't you see how it works?" asked Betty. "Suppose you are in that awful maze of discordant elements that is our world of limited sight, where you can't understand values and get confused over issues. You can't distinguish the right thing to do. So you go aside and throw your heart and soul into spiritual association. You lift up your capacity to receive. The union of strength makes a shaft of power and light, and you turn it on your problem. Thus you see clearly."

"You not only do that," added the Invisible, "but you gain strength to walk in that path, and to pursue it to the very end of your vista."

Another by-product, if it can be considered that, is a much more profound experience.

"You can," said Betty, speaking of this, "conceive a spiritual being by the strength of your desire for contact.

You do it just by calling for spiritual companionship and association. But this amounts to very little unless something arises within you to enlarge your capacity to receive it and blend with it.

"Something within you must rise continually to meet the spiritual association," she repeated. "You don't just wait for it to come to you. Weak prayer does not fulfill its part because it just calls down, instead of rising to meet."

"Prayer," put in the Invisible, "is the projection of your spiritual being, heart and soul. It is the conscious assembling of your higher self. In offering up the spirit, you lay bare your own soul. It is the only way you can recognize your own spiritual proportions; you then face the sum total of yourself. It pierces all your coverings and trappings as an X-ray pierces the body. There is a terrible reality to it.

"This is its ultimate action, this compulsion to

face your naked soul.

"From dread of this, people use only the surface of prayer. But there is no discouragement with this facing; no discouragement. Even mortification is submerged in eagerness to reconstruct and harmonize. This is the big feeling prayer gives you. You must plumb the depths of prayer down to your timid soul in order to gain impetus.

"Under the inspiration of prayer each one of us recognizes the *wholeness* necessary to spiritual harmony. In proportion as he lacks is the urge to acquire the wholeness he perceives."[*]

In view of this description one of us asked if, then, the element of supplication in prayer is erroneous.

"Prayer," replied the Invisible, "is in essence a complete conscious unfoldment of self for the reception of the vivifying, healing and developing influence of spirit. Conscious unfoldment means necessarily a clear-eyed, honest, impersonal understanding of one's self. The conscious fact of this understanding acts as though it removed a barrier against the germinating waters. Until such acknowledgment, those waters are prevented by that barrier from their nourishment office. In that conception there is no room for a demand for specific favors beyond the demand made by acknowledgment of

---

[*] Once again, as in the Chapter on Meditation, all these quotations must be taken in supplement to the discussion of the subject in the other books. See *The Betty Book*, pages 133-141; *Anchors to Windward*, pages 110, 143, 158, 161; *The Stars Are Still There*, pages 102, 105, 121-2, 145. 154-5, 157.

a lack in yourself."

"I am wondering," one of us speculated, "about the wisdom of using the word 'prayer' at all. It has become so overlaid with narrower meanings."

"I think," said Betty, "that most people understand, at least dimly, what prayer is."

"I'm not so sure," insisted the other. "In most minds it means an attempt to influence a power beyond you in your behalf. Usually it is just a petition directed to a god, something with a magic power to answer. It seems to me we need some different word to express the kind of contact you describe."

"The majority of people," said the Invisible, "cannot aspire to such contact; their evolution is not high enough. Nevertheless, the formulation of a need into a thought, a petition, with the sure submerging of self that comes with prayer to what is higher and greater than self, is beneficent to the individual."

— 2 —

One traditional point of difficulty about prayer is the confusion between the ideas of going to the Source directly or through an intermediary. It is a fundamental divergence, for example, between the Catholic and the Protestant systems. But may not both views be correct? And need the approach be invariable? Might it not be one or the other according to conditions? And is a hard and fast decision really important? The Invisibles did not seem to think so. "First we go to our Source, of course. That is the first step. The intermediary aspect is the *second* step. One can dispense with it, but only if he is master enough to supply, all by himself, sufficient human warmth and love for his fellow beings so that a channel is made for the flow of spiritual force. Without that channel there is a gap between the sensing of the power and the utilizing of the power in affairs.

"This is badly expressed," the Invisible admitted. "Our urge is to take the impersonal chill out of what is called spirituality. It is ordinarily set apart for rarefied moments. We would make it a warm pulsing spiritual blood stream that will keep us healthy; that will warm us, and flush us with quick responses."

Another time they laid more emphasis on the intermediary aspect and explained more fully its importance in the scheme of things.

"The contribution," said they, "of any individual to any occasion is his transmutation into assimilable form of his intake of power from the Source. That is the function of the individual as respects his environment. If any one is to help by the power he receives, it must be by transmutation of that power in terms of his own genius. This you have already understood.

"But these things you have not considered: that those on whom you thus bestow receive also themselves from the Source; and that what they receive from you is not the pure power from the Source, but your transmutation of it; and that your contribution is in the nature of a supplement to their own degree of direct intake.

"Also you have not considered this: that in

relation to those who can bestow upon you, you stand in the same place as those upon whom you bestow.

"Therefore, in reaching for emergency assistance, you must not only open your channel to its widest and freest intake from the Source. You would do well also to call specifically for help upon those whose transmutations fit that necessity.

"To be sure, many of us have remained without name, but you know well how to distinguish us. And if you should bethink you, you can call in recollection hosts of those who have preceded you, and who are warm to you and eager to bring help if called upon. But that eagerness cannot avail without the definite and personal appeal. We cannot answer needs, only desires. Each of us is capable of help in his own way, so that if you bethink you of John, who had gaiety, and ask him personally – as one would ask any friend for his help – he will bring you gladly the sustainment of the light heart. And so, cast you in your mind to all those you know with us here, and call to them, saying, 'I am in need of sustainment. Come you, my dear friend, to my aid.' Then the way is opened, and you are rejoicingly surrounded.

"I mean this literally. Call you the roll, dwelling on each with a personal call, and hold him in the reviving warmth of recollection, so that the color of each will glow in your heart. This little ceremony is an enablement, lacking which they must yearn mute without the barrier.

"In this you see, perhaps, a justification of those who talk of the intercession of the saints; nor in kind does it differ, for saints are those made known to a for some quality of transmuting for common use. Sainthood is not a peculiar and exalted state. It is merely a designation by human authority of certain ones considered strong enough in development to answer a general call. As to saintSHIP, you stand yourself in that state when, on rare occasion, you are privileged to stoop and bless."

The Invisible here added a corollary to the law of complement.

"That help of this personal sort may not always respond, is part of wisdom. If your child calls for your sustaining hand upon the wide pleasances of a lawn, he meets your denial; because then, even if he stumble, he will learn to walk alone. But if he must cross the thronged highway, he may reach to you in confidence of response.

"In like manner, when you come to a highway which you must cross, many hands are reached in eagerness, waiting but that you raise your arm. So content you not alone with reaching toward the pure power from the Source, but permit to gather around you the eagerly proffered bucklers of your own people. And weary not in your calling, for the humblest companion of your past has some small gift of strength or joyousness which he alone can fashion, and which itself alone can fulfill. Nor is there in all cosmos one whom you think too great for your summoning. We here are overburdened with gifts we would bestow. When you call upon us, even the greatest, you are bestowing upon us a privilege; for on your earth, though needs are as the sands of the shore, the opportunities of our meeting them are rare as cries in a great wilderness."

— 3 —

The following are a few of the formulated prayers given us from time to time by the Invisibles:

PRAYER FOR ABUNDANCE

'To him who hath given so much we make supplication. Pour upon us thy strength that we may receive our allotment, and give us in thy name of thy abundance. Let us walk with thee in spirit, partaking of thy divine mind. For knowledge and wisdom and growth in harmony with thy laws we this day do make our demand. As we are fit to receive give of thy abundance, Father of all.'

"Next time," concluded the Invisible, "you walk alone in darkness use this prayer to dispel the shadows. Keep it as a magic to give you power to fight your way up into the fight again."

PRAYER FOR THE FULNESS OF LIFE

This was offered by Betty, perhaps more an aim, a wish, than a prayer.

"Give me all of life before I leave, all! I don't want a niche. Aren't there plenty of people to fill niches? Of course they are happier in the peace of limited struggle. I want most tremendously and vehemently the highest possible comprehension. I want to take the suffering and all; I don't care if it tears me to bits; I want it! I've made my choice: I don't care if it is hard. Besides, it isn't all that. The intensification of living, alone, is worth it."

And again, later, another expression of the same desire:

"I want to get nearer, nearer to the source of all striving life. I want to smell the wet earth and feel the coot drip of rocks. I want to sway with the presence of the wind. That is all life, life. What gives us that quality? I want to keep close, close, close as I can get to that. I want to sniff it, taste it, drink it, bathe in it. That's where I want to be. I don't like the dead things. Some people like intellectual conquest, mechanical things, making automatons; but I don't like it. I crave the live things; things endowed with self-structure.

"I want to get near enough so I can partake of the same great vitality. Throw open all hatches; it's stale. I want to go out in the wind and the light and the air. I don't know what you call that current of vitality... Never mind its name; I'm going to get close to it."

"Here," said the Invisible, meeting this desire, is a prayer:

"I am the heir of eternal expansion and clothed in my right to partake of it. I am expanding to participate in the gorgeous fullness of it. There is no possible expression for the fullness and rhythm. Oh do not let me ever again be poor-spirited or faded or gnarled in form. I want the richly patterned life. I want to be gorgeous-spirited. I want the ceremonial beauty and fragrance of the spirit. I want the freedom of its force. I want the quiet whispering of its wisdom. I want the simplicity of its love. Oh give me, help me to the fullness of life. Oh keep me from starving myself. Give me liberty to be a quickener to others. Do not let me sink in inertia. I pray now for the fullness of life with an undivided heart, so that I may rest absorbed in strength, not emptying myself of life!"

A PRAYER FOR HELP IN HEALING

"Melt; blend; receive without effort, but with the gratefulness earth offers to the rain." The Invisibles were speaking of the contact.

This mantra you may say silently within yourself when by meditation you have entered into power:

"'God is comfort. I call on him who is most in comfort to bring comfort to this one.

"'God is pity. I call on him who is most in pitifulness to bestow pity on this one.

"'God is strength. I call on him who is most in strength to bring strength to this one.

"'God is healing. I call on him who is most in healing to bring healing to this one.

"'For myself. To that degree to which I have purely come to use of God, use me for these purposes.'"

XI Harmony

AS SOON as you begin to live in the truth that you hold all power within you, new worlds will open up in all directions like magic.

INVISIBLE

— 1 —

IN THE communion implied by meditation, and especially prayer, we are entering a state of being wherein some of the solidly material correspondences of everyday life yield more or less to certain imponderables. We cease to deal with the body and its concerns; we associate and work with what we have called the distillations, the essences. These essences are the raw material, it seems, with which one deals in the unobstructed aspect of the universe, *whether we are here or there.*

Betty early recognized this truth and expressed it, though the rest of us did not fully grasp the implications until she herself had gone to the unobstructed universe, and reported back that trilogy of essences which has so engaged the thinking scientific world.

"You see," said she, while she was still here, "I must begin to collect some materials for myself. If I am to work in essences this way – between the pure spiritual conception and its manifestation – I must get the tools of my craft. So I must collect myself essences:

the time-achievement of the tree; the energy of my waterfalls; the stability in my rock. The sweet chemistry of earth is endless. All I have to do is to walk in my garden collecting and releasing essences, never hoarding in the cloistered-garden sense. Essences are everywhere to work with. It needs only the sensitive heart to utilize them."

Only after she left us were we given the basic hypothesis.

It is too complicated to lay out fully here. I must refer you to the book.[*] Perhaps its essence can be well enough expressed by quotation from the record.

"The constant of consciousness is a trilogia consisting of absolute motion, absolute space, absolute time. The greatest of these is time. Now each has a primary property, or essence.

"The essence of absolute motion is frequency. The essence of absolute space is conductivity. The essence of absolute time is receptivity.

"All operate in the absolute of their constant aspects in orthos.

"We give you this new term – orthos (as in orthodoxy, orthochromatic, etc), which is the Greek word for true. Now the term orthos simply means the true, constant characteristic of the reality, consciousness. Your empirical knowledge has taught you that in the obstructed universe there are three

---

[*] *The Unobstructed Universe.*

dimensions. We have told you that there is an orthic trilogia – in other words, three characteristics of consciousness that always obtain. These three are orthic time, orthic space, and orthic motion. They are the three greatest familiars of your obstructed universe; and also of the entire universe.

"Now we have chosen the word 'essence' as a term in this new exposition, to be used in its basic meaning. The essence of orthic time is receptivity; the essence of sidereal time is receptivity. The essence of orthic space is conductivity; the essence of sidereal space is conductivity. The essence of orthic motion is frequency; the essence of sidereal motion is frequency.

"The new thought that has been growing in your consciousness is the fact that the three essences of the orthic trilogia – receptivity, conductivity and frequency – have been manifested in the obstructed universe as time, space and motion, precisely as consciousness itself has manifested in the obstructed universe as man, nature and matter."

These "essences" of the things with which we are already familiar here in our earth life, Betty assures us from her present vantage in the unobstructed, are the everyday material for activity in the invisible life.

"I told you once that over here I worked in essences," said she, "I spoke of 'going around my garden collecting essences.' You will find it in one of the books and in the records. That is how I work now – in essences. But I live, as always, in an actual world. Now:

"The *essences* of Time plus Space plus Motion

138

equals created matter of some kind, depending on their proportions, etc. Thus we have the constituents of a world – yours or mine, or other worlds beyond ours.

"The essences of Time plus Space equals duration." (If you inject Space into pure Time you get the extension of time to duration.)

"The essences of Space plus Time equals distance." (If you inject into space the "slowness" of getting there, you lave distance.)

"The essences of Motion plus Space equals pure communication." (There is in radio a slight injection of time, of course; but that comes nearest to "pure communication" with us.)

"The essences of Motion plus Time equals pure Being."

She went on to explain her manipulations in dealing with her kind of space and time, but that aspect of the subject is complicated and beside our purpose. The point is that she can manipulate them according to their nature and her own skill. What affects our present argument is her conclusion.

"Less completely, within my capability of dealing with the pure essence, I can approach the state of pure Being. Impossible to do so perfectly. That is an ultimate. Matter of growth and development. Principle only."

— 2 —

What is this pure Being of which Betty speaks? According to her statement it awaits us at the end of the road. An ultimate. As such it must concern our proposed self-development. The Invisibles agreed this was true. But also they wanted to know what we meant by "self."

"Self," one of us ventured, "is my inward feeling of being, as distinct from any feeling of awareness at all."

"Yes," the Invisible approved, "this feeling of being is the essence of self. Now this self that can take cognizance of an inside and outside world we might define as Being. What is its importance?

"The simplest form in which the sum total can be put is this: the pure sensation of what we have called Being is the fundamental essence of eternal life; you must accustom your emotional nature to accept and practice and deeply groove your habits to indulge the strength of this Being; only so will you acquire the functioning higher consciousness awaiting you, the true spiritual body, as gratifying material as the one you now occupy."

"In all ways possible," said Betty, "I am going to attack this deliberate acquisition of higher consciousness. Its negative side is recognized as acquisition of power. But pure Being is not a sum to be added up. It is a continuous outgoing thing, like radio-active force. The withholding of the laws of this force has been necessitated through its misapprehension in terms of acquisition of power. It is so perilously easy to slide into your world terms, your visible tangible terms of acquisition of power, in dealing with intangible higher potentialities. It has retarded the race in past centuries.

"The practice of this sensation of Being," continued the Invisible, "is of such importance that, regardless of the absurdities of inept language incapable of containing the concept, we will repeatedly struggle to introduce it as a functioning reality. It is the great magnetic clement without which you are not aware of the availability of the creative process of the universe."

— **3** —

This sensation of timeless Being, existing solely in the sensation of Now, was touched upon in the chapter on Meditation. It is, we were told, akin to pure Feeling; though at first Betty felt she must defend the term as too full of emotional connotations.

"Some day I'm going to take pure Feeling and cleanse it of the taint of transient emotion, weak sentiment, because pure Feeling is the divine spark. It is the intelligence of the heart, the secret of creative magic. Pure Feeling is a warrior quality. It is made of the stuff that endures. Strong and true it engages with earth passions and hatreds and comes through them unscathed. It is somewhat as an adult feels protectingly toward a kicking, screaming child rescued from adventuring on the dangerous road. I despair of setting down pure Feeling, or finding words to contain it. "Pure Feeling alone can guide you safely. That is the highest desirability of life – pure Feeling. The race has always touched it in its great moments. Conscious understanding of it has lacked. It is the combination, the perfect blend, of spiritual inflow with earth embodiment and function. It triumphs over all physical tensions. You have but to feel deeply and happily to perceive this for yourself. It is as if the solids of you became as a radiating intangible substance.

"You can cultivate pure Feeling by welcoming its entrance into your heart region. Experiment, and see how it softens all the cruel rigidities of life, how it escapes all chains and shackles of maladjustments. This inner flame is one of the most silently apparent of possessions. It makes its way without words or exhibition. It travels from heart to heart in its own channels of expression and exchange. It is a reciprocal thing. We sense it, even if we do not acknowledge it with anything better than mental sophistication, as toward something simple folk and peasants have. Too great development on the mental side does not admit the need of pure Feeling. It is looked on as dangerous to logic. Could pure Feeling be allowed natural development to the point where it would nourish what we recognize as intellect, then we would have man as he is intended to be, as he is now in moments of devotion to ideals."

— 4 —

Pure Being and pure Feeling stand high on our list of importances. Perhaps at the very top. But also, avowedly, they are ultimates, and as such can be of little immediate value to us. If we are to put them to practical use, we must have some sort of handhold with which to grasp them. The Invisibles recognized this.

"Any human experience," they explained, "no matter what its nature, no matter what its inception, no matter what its guiding influence, may be analyzed into two elements. They are a reality which is its core and substance; and its interpretation, which may be deed or thought. The core of reality must always exist, for if a thing is in this orderly universe, it must have back of it an indubitable real essence. The interpretation varies according to circumstance. In the most harmonious adjustment it may approach a comparative correspondence, and in any case will encompass what may be called a working correspondence. In circumstances involving maladjustment, or activities mistaken, the core of truth may be so overlaid with uncorresponding interpretations as to suffer almost complete falsification. In the simplest direct working of an accomplished evolution the interpretation may bear to the reality almost an equalizing ratio."

Such a core of reality, by definition, is pure Being. Our job, then, is to find a satisfactory interpretation into ordinary everyday terms. Betty had a suggestion or two to point the way.

"Examples of pure Being," said she, "are such things as light and heat and energy, which are first, and *manifest* second. Love; humor; interested creation of the kind one does pleasurably; all the unobstructed channels of everyday life endowed with ease and richness of output – these are aspects of pure Being."

Another time the Invisibles gave us a more complete insight. The word "harmony," they explained, is the best clue to a practical interpretation of pure Being.

"Harmony," they defined, "is not an attitude of action toward externals. It is a state of being.

"You can recognize it as such if you will recall some fragment of life divested of all but simplicities – not that a state of harmony depends upon such a divestment: but merely to get an understanding of the pure quality. Hark back within your experience to some time when, for a greater or lesser period – a month, a week, a day, even an hour – life has seemed so simplified as to flow forward without the necessity of impulse, and without the constrainment of taking thought; with no time appointments to meet, with no dutiful calls to answer, and yet not devoid of the activities natural and appropriate to that spiritual spaciousness. At such times has it not seemed to you, perhaps, that you experienced a certain overflow beyond the boundaries of your workaday tight personality, to include a kinship with those things about you that are pacing with you in like rhythm? So that, whatever happens, you move toward and through events with a certain satisfied inevitability, with no apprehension, and equally with no externalized appreciation, accepting their occurrence as you accept your indrawn breath?

"You must divorce this simple, pure state of Being from whatever ecstasy or mentally acknowledged happiness or intellectually considered appreciation you may experience. These may, indeed, sometimes be off-shoots or concomitants of the state of Being, but are not of its prime substance. And, of course, we are assuming for the purpose, I am reminding you, a space of time at which the sharp-toothed demands of life have not gnawed.

"This picture is presented so that you may perhaps recognize in, its uttermost simplicity the state of Being which we call harmony. It is a flowing, not a static contentment. That is the underlying structure of a life attuned, in whatever degree. Overlaid is the substance of life itself."

XII The Point of Reference

CONDITIONS can seldom be ideal. Make them at least conquerable.

INVISIBLE

— 1 —

WE HAVE talked a lot about reality; but do we know what it is?

"*Consciousness*," said the Invisibles, "is the one and only reality." Whether or not we apprehend the full truth of the statement, we feel it by instinct – the instinct for expansion of awareness which underlies all human effort. The longing for reality is why we undertake the efforts and exercises outlined in the preceding pages. A fundamental necessity is first of all to establish a core of it in ourselves, an "inner fortress" as Betty said, impregnably our own.

So basic is this instinct, so impelling the urge for reality, that certain errors of thought have arisen and solidified. We can be satisfied with nothing less than reality, the argument goes. Analysis shows us that externals are merely manifestations, interpretations. Therefore, if we are to come to reality, we must get rid of externals.

This is an over-simplification of course, but it is the reasoning back of the Oriental systems that emphasize negation for the riddance of "Illusion"; of the Occidental systems that refuse ugly facts of life on the general principle that God is good and therefore the ugliness and evil have no genuine existence. In either case the first steps toward merit must be to rid ourselves of deception. To do so we must deny the reality of things in the world in order to reach the reality of consciousness. Since there exists in humankind an equally strong instinct of affinity for our enjoyable material surroundings, we have a conflict.

As is often the case, the difficulty is largely one of terminology. We are trying to use the same word for two different concepts. We must learn to distinguish; to stop saying reality when what we mean is actuality. Consciousness is the one and only reality, all-containing, all-inclusive, the origin and core of all there is. Reality we contain in degree according to our capacity – which is sometimes pretty small. But we are composed of and surrounded by what we should call actualities. They, too, share in the qualities of all-consciousness, *each according to its capacity of the moment.* So they are not intrinsically real, no matter how actual they are to us. But that does not mean they are illusion, "maya." They contain the quality of reality, or not, according to our point of reference to them.

— **2** —

That is obscure in thought; and not too easy to clarify. Perhaps the best approach would be to remind ourselves that Science postulates exactly the same thing!

There is no reality to the world about you, says the Eastern type of mysticism. All is illusion, maya, and

147

if you would set foot on the path you must first of A rid yourself of illusion by denial and "mortification of the flesh." Only thus can you gain spiritual integrity.

There is no reality in the world about you, says Science. What you call the real things analyze down through atom, molecule, proton, neutron, electron to pure force. You are simply fooled by the senses; and you'd better revise your idea that things are solid if you value your intellectual integrity.

Both the mystic and the scientist in one respect stand on the same platform; illusion is to them synonymous with futility, ergo, if you want to amount to anything, the sooner you deny any reality to the things about you, the more quickly you will touch ultimate truth.

The argument looks to be watertight until we examine another word. This appears to be largely an affair of semantics. In this case the word is *ultimate*.

Who ever had the nerve to start the idea that we can deal with ultimates – of truth or anything else? We can envisage intellectually some ultimates, but we cannot live them. Why? *Because We Are Not Ourselves Ultimates*. Possibly the aim of evolution is toward that, but right now is the immediate, and we ourselves are immediates, surrounded by immediates with which we have to deal. They are actual – not illusory – *at our point of reference to them.*

Here is a chair in which I am sitting. As an ultimate – philosophical or scientific – it can be said to have no actuality; it is either a nexus of pure force or it is an idea in consciousness. Nevertheless, it supports me. No amount of argument can disprove to me that it is "real" enough to hold me up. It is only when I choose to consider the chair as a phenomenon of physics, rather than a device of utility, that my point of reference to it shifts, and its "reality" drains from it.

So we come tentatively to a principle, do we not? Actuality is not an affair of the thing-itself; it is a relationship. And it is a shifting relationship. Quite genuinely a thing may be "real" or a delusion according to the observer's or the user's point of reference to it. Or to put it another way, more pictorially, actuality is a quality of universal consciousness which can fill any container – or depart from it – according to conditions. So it is entirely possible for the chair to be for me "real" because my point of reference to it is as a support, and to be for the physicist an illusion because at the moment his point of reference to it is in the laboratory.

Obviously, if we accept that as a provisional hypothesis, we must admit that the point of reference is more or less movable. The physicist can sit down in the chair and find it solid. It is indubitable that he has a selective power that can place its actuality where it will, within his limitations of course. All of us possess that privilege. It is part of our heritage of free-will. The width of field through which we can shift our point of reference depends on the width of our understanding. We can establish no point of reference with a thing that is unknown to us, and no *effective* point of reference with a thing we do not comprehend. We can acknowledge that such a thing has actuality; but that is merely an intellectual acknowledgment of belief in some authority who does understand. It makes for us no solid actuality. A Southern Cracker wholly ignorant of physics could establish no actuality, no point of reference, with the neutron-proton-electron constitution of matter, though he may admit "it is so if you say so." He fails to do so simply because he has no understanding of what it is all about.

Since, thus, the power of selecting our points of reference widens as we grow, the higher our degree of development, the more "real" are we capable of making things, the more inclusive will be our understanding, the farther out or along are we capable of establishing points of reference.

— **3** —

So we all, to a degree, have a choice as to where, at the moment, we want a thing to be actual, or "real." To continue with our physicist, he can elect to refer himself to the chair as something to sit on, in which case it is to him an actual chair; or he may prefer to refer himself to it as a laboratory matter, in which case it ceases to exist for him as a chair, and the actuality moves into his fresh point of reference. Sometimes the shift possible is a wide one. That, as we have said, depends on a man's education and development. But while this wide shift exists for him, nonetheless he has an *average* point of reference to things, which determines for him the actuality of his world. And that, in a fashion, results in a variety of worlds. The average point of reference of the astronomer, for instance, is far removed from the average point of reference of the fellow whose business it is to build concrete dams or bridges. Note the word "average." The astronomer is quite capable of a point of reference to dams and bridges that will bring them into reality to him – when he wants to cross them. The builder can focus on the atoms and the stars on suitable occasion. But in his normal occupation, construction work simply does not exist for one; nor stars in the daytime for the other.

And note this: in a normal and balanced life any man's level of his habitual point of reference is that level which is the most effective functioning of that man. If he habitually finds his actualities – his points of reference – above or below the level of his normal life, he becomes more or less futile. And certainly unadjusted and hence unhappy. And if his actualities are far enough removed from that average level, he is tucked away in an asylum. Not that the insane man has no genuine actualities in his life – as is the common belief – but that they are too remote. What might be called the basic realities of living are with him shifted outside the common human environment. Life cannot function effectively; and there you have, from the practical standpoint, "delusion and futility."

The displacement of this man, like others who talk more sanely of ultimate truth, is an example of trying to deal with ultimates before becoming ultimate. We deal with immediates, simply because we are ourselves immediate. With them we establish our points of reference; and at once, when we do so, they are "real."

Parenthetically, if accepting a point of reference can bestow actuality on its object, so deliberate denying a point of reference can relegate it to nullity. And that could be very useful.

XIII Manifestation

FINITE manifestation is, in conception, an idea. An idea, in rounded wholeness, is an harmonious arrangement. An harmonious arrangement is a product of creative imagination, Creative imagination is an attribute of intelligence.

INVISIBLE

— 1 —

WE HAVE examined functioning, its incentives, its ingredients, the necessity for it if the individual is to develop in his evolution. We have not stopped to observe that identically the same processes and necessities that obtain with the individual consciousness govern also Consciousness as manifested in the finite universe. It, too, is in evolution, for though in the finite the all-inclusive perfection of All Consciousness obtains – as it must – all-inclusiveness in that aspect is merely of *potential* that must be brought out and developed to become to us actuality. Exactly as with the individual, this can be done only by functioning. In this case, clearly, functioning means creation. In the individual, though not so clearly, the same is true. We will take that up later. Meantime we will only note that both in the cosmic and in the individual, one basic, inborn, irresistible urge is the instinct for creation.

Let us examine the creative process as it goes on in the finite universe we know. Possibly this will help us to understand better our own personal effort.

— 2 —

We are concerned now merely with method. For the moment the philosophical and metaphysical aspects are irrelevant. The ultimate Purpose of it all is not a matter for our speculation. We interest ourselves only with what is actually going on. A brief outline will do for a starter. We begin, then, with the all-embracing power that is the All-Consciousness, our one and only reality. In the finite – which is all we can deal with – it is pure force, undifferentiated. Its urge is toward differentiation, for which another word is manifestation. Manifestation of pure undifferentiated force *of any kind* is possible only by the interposition of resistance.

Let us pause for a moment to consider that last statement. It is not as unfamiliar as it sounds. This room is all the time full of the pure force of radio broadcast, which becomes manifest only when I interpose the mechanism of my radio set. Electricity remains undisclosed until it becomes light or power or heat according to the kind of resistance thrown across its flow. And so on. It will be found to be a general law.

The only way, originally, that resistance can be interposed is by intelligence. I use the word "originally" because otherwise someone would be sure to object that in later processes the checking by resistance may be purely a mechanical intervention of laws. But in the beginning the laws themselves must be seen to be a product of intelligence.

— 3 —

That is the statement in a nutshell. The Invisibles presented it more in detail, and from many different angles of approach. On one such occasion we had been discussing a curious phenomenon with our friend Margaret Cameron.* She had discovered that she could induce between her hands, apparently at will, what seemed to be a current of force. This she had used for certain types of healing, and in the process had noted an interesting thing. The current

was not always the same. In fact, it varied considerably. Sometimes it felt hot, sometimes cold, sometimes prickly. It was this variation we had been discussing. Were these, we wondered, actually different forces?

"It is all one force," declared the Invisible. "It is a differentiation for especial purposes of the one stream of vitality which flows ceaselessly through all cosmos. This is evident only when arrested, or rather slowed up, when it becomes either visible or palpable or effective, through the efforts of its dynamics to free itself and proceed upon its way. Arrested by an *idea* it becomes a creature or a thing, dependent for its form and its attributes upon the nature of the idea, what we have called the quality of consciousness. Slowed up by a purpose, rather than an idea, it becomes a vehicle of differentiated force, dependent for its nature and its effect upon the nature of the purpose.

"The origin of the idea that results in the created thing is an intelligence of higher development than your

---

* Author of *The Seven Purposes*.

own or my own. Such intelligence as ours, however, can construct a purpose which may be effective. The handling and originating of these purposes is the essential of the technique of utilizing these currents of force."

As to the nature of this primary "force," this flow of vitality, another Invisible had to say:

"Now let's see. This force. Its nature is to dissipate, unless it meets some force that helps its particularization. But the force *wants* to be assisted, so to speak. It comes for the purpose of obtaining complementary force. I don't want to speak didactically, but I must build a little fence of words around the conception. So remember that: remember there is a waiting undifferentiated thing that wants to be differentiated."

What results from this differentiation – which is a checking by an intention, to use an inclusive term, originating in intelligence – is a creation of some sort. What that creation is depends on the intention, or plan. No thing can possibly exist in the material except *after* it has existed in plan. That is true of original creation; it is also true of even our simplest fabrication. If we are going to build a chair, we must first plan its details in our minds. We have been told that the 64 plans," or prototypes, in the Invisible of the various species of earth may be called *qualities of consciousness*. That bit of Consciousness which is manifested as a tree does so because it has treeness as its quality. The dog is a dog because he is an embodiment of the dog quality of Consciousness. So likewise with the human and the reptile and the mineral and all that is. Each represents its own quality of Consciousness. And, to return to the starting point, that quality is what it is because the flow of primal force has been checked, or slowed, or arrested by that *intention*.

"The very grass you walk on supports the argument. Grass is the effect of force, the current of Life differentiated and purposed in the direction of grass – checked into manifestation, but defined as the intention of grass. By the same process and for the same reason, you are you. The thing that is you is an arrestment of motion, the essence of which is frequency. Your frequency is what you are, just as an arrestment of another frequency makes the tree."

"By arrestment I do not mean stoppage. Take the supposition that matter is a rate of vibration. There is a rate of movement that represents matter. Since there is only one Reality, and as matter is one thing and you another, you must have different rates of vibration. The essence of both you and matter is consciousness. The difference between you and matter is the rate of vibration, *the frequency*. But the nature of frequency is motion. Therefore, everything is in motion. That is why consciousness and the universe are in evolution."

This precipitated a question which plunged us into a discussion of the *essences* of our finite time, space and motion: which were defined, it will be recalled, as receptivity, conductivity and frequency.[*]

"About the arresting of frequencies," said one of us, "what *does* the arresting – mechanically, I mean?"

---

[*] For a discussion of the constitution of matter, see *The Unobstructed Universe,* from which some of this is quoted.

"The juxtaposition of frequencies in time and space. You could perhaps illustrate it by algebra. X plus Y plus Z equals a stone. X plus 2Y plus Z equals a weed. 2X plus Y plus Z equals a flower. And so on. X is a frequency; Y is a conductivity; Z is a receptivity."

"That describes a process," objected the questioner, "but does not say what does the arresting. And anyway I don't like the word 'arrest.' That means stop short. A frequency's got to wiggle a little."

"The potentiality of evolution is still in the arrested frequency. It is held in suspension," was the reply to this.

"Nevertheless, what arrests the frequency?" we persisted.

"Here is a line coming down on a slant this way; call it receptivity. Here's a line coming down on a slant this way; call that conductivity. And here's a line slanting in still another way; and we'll call that frequency. Now all three are in evolution. If the lines of frequency and conductivity strike receptivity together in one place, one manifestation occurs. If you move the angle the first two make so they strike the third in even the slightest deviation from the former position, then you get another manifestation. But always all three must come together at a single point. They are variable, malleable and in evolution."

"Frequencies coming into time and space are arrested by the very nature of that situation?" we asked further.

"No. It occurs because there is a stress point created by the juxtaposition of the three. Varying angles of incidence; various stress points."

These general principles seemed to us clear enough. The Invisibles evidently considered that sufficient had been given to warrant an epitome.

"I will make an attempt, now that all the evidence has been stated piecemeal, to sketch a picture of the whole process of creative fashioning.

"The infinite universe is a flow of unbroken and unmanifested harmony. Creation is an arrestment or checking of the flow of this universal harmony, its differentiation, and its rearrangement into a new form of particularization.

"The amount and the quality of this first segregation is dependent on the interposition of an individual entity by which it is checked and through which it is filtered.

"The rearrangement depends upon the innate creative imagination possessed by that entity.

"The endurance of the result is dependent on the dynamics with which the creative intelligence works. These dynamics in turn depend upon the degree of spiritual development and aspiration to which their originator has attained.

"The reality of the creation – reality in its broadest sense – is closely related to the fact that both the fashioning and the embodiment are carried out through a finite medium. I use the word 'finite' in place of 'material,' though in the broad sense the two terms are interchangeable. However, common acceptance has given the word 'material' a narrower connotation.

"These are all the elements, collected together and stated, of the creative act."

— **4** —

We have considered the general principles of creation. There remains to examine the particularized manifestations – all the million and one physical constituents of the universe. Each is as it is because of its individual and unique frequency. That unique frequency represents a specific quality of that Consciousness which is the one reality. Its manifestation on earth is the product of intelligence. That is as far as we have gone.

But admitting this, why, since Consciousness is actually all of its qualities, does it manifest, at this moment or this place, one of them rather than another? Is that, too, on the judgment and choice of guiding intelligence? Or is it part of some more or less mechanical process of evolution?

This problem was called to our attention in the midst of an Invisible discourse on Qualities.

"The stream of life, or quality, or spirit," the Invisible was saying "might be said to flow by continuously. In every drop of that current is *everything there is* – not only every quality, but every element of every quality. From these qualities every individual thing that comes into existence is born.

"Now it is likely that you may have formed in your minds an image of qualities as separate pools or reservoirs. This is not unnatural, when you consider the almost infinite multiplicity of qualities of Consciousness that must lie back of their innumerable manifestations. But this is a misconception.

"To be sure, the qualities of Consciousness are distinct – each in itself a complete whole, containing all the elements comprising itself. But with full appreciation of that fact, you must accustom yourself to the idea of these qualities as so interfused throughout all cosmos that we may literally say each pin point of space contains in itself *all elements of all qualities of consciousness.*"

'While we were discussing this point one of our group had a dismaying idea. She did not express it, but the Invisible caught the idea, and chuckled.

"Mrs. L.," he explained to the rest of us, "is disturbed by the statement that all quality is everywhere present unsegregated. She sees no reason why we should not then have bullfrogs everywhere. I would tell her this:

"The law of manifestation is in no way different from any other law. It acts only when the conditions are assembled, of the right kind and in proper proportion. The reason that tree quality, say, manifests itself at any given point in space, is not because the tree quality is especially more present there than elsewhere. It is

160

because the conditions for the manifestation of tree quality are there present more strongly than are the conditions for any other quality.

"This being the case, it is natural to ask why one condition, or set of conditions, obtains at one particular place rather than another. To answer that question we must first of all examine the method of the working of any law whatever.

"No man ever causes a law to act. He merely assembles in proper juxtaposition and proportion the necessary conditions. Having done so, he cannot *prevent* the law from acting. You think you light the fire. As a matter of fact, you pile your wood; you place your kindling; you insert the paper. You then supply the chemical, under those conditions of motion and abrasion, to the oxygenation of those materials. The law steps in.

"Who or what gathers together in like manner the conditions necessary to the production or manifestation of your tree quality or whatever quality? The same thing in essence which has gathered together the fire material – Intelligence.

"There is no working of any law unless the conditions for that law are arranged. And that arrangement comes through Intelligence. You may – if you would quibble – point to the gathering of certain conditions by the action of certain laws, but that is only pushing the subject back. In the final analysis you will still discover – Intelligence."

And in final summing up:

"All this that we have said applies to all the created work in the finite universe, as it has evolved to its present state of development, from the simplest of material elements to the highest response-mechanisms of the All Conscious in finite embodiment These things have been created by intelligence, self-evolved. Anything that intelligence makes is fashioned by these methods. One of the most important and responsible objects of your own creative powers is yourself. That method, in that task also, you employ. You employ it in every moment that is actually creative. That method, and that method alone, is your tool for the fashioning of your whole life as well, now and forever after, until, in the mysterious rounding to a conclusion of whatever the Great Purpose may be, your handiwork will be fitted into the finite Completion. Therefore, study it well; for its application, and the comfortableness of its assurance, is fitting to all occasion.

"Now we have finished."

XIV Our Part in Creation

Every true spark you strike from out your own soul is a light that has not shone before and that shall never be extinguished.

INVISIBLE

SO-CALLED malevolent and evil creations are but extreme examples of incompleteness. They are ugly because they are partial. Completed, they will be seen as the lesser curves of a beautiful whole.

INVISIBLE

— **1** —

AGREED that self-development is our primary creative function, plainly it is not our one and only. Too many other instances throng forward when we examine our lives. For example, when we do so simple a thing as to plant a nasturtium seed, we have afforded the life force an opportunity it would not otherwise have bad to express itself in manifestation. It is within our power to bestow or withhold that one chance.

That is one of our simplest roles in creation. Likewise we can in various ways interpose resistances across the undifferentiated flow of the vital force which will check it to tangibility. Many of these are purely mechanical and impersonal, as in the case of the safety match and the electric generator. But there is also the realm of the thinker and the artist and the inventor – and even more intimately, the worker in pure spiritual substance. A man's ability in this field is limited only by his capacity to receive and conduct the vital force from the Source, and to particularize it for a purpose. For that is the creative process, whether he uses it instinctively and blindly and blunderingly – as is most often the case – or with the knowledge and intelligence to which he is slowly evolving.

Our true importance to the scheme of things in this connection is not apparent to the casual eye. The Invisibles underscored this apropos of someone's request for direct advice.

"Precipitation on the physical plane," said they, "must come from those endowed with physical faculties. It must be a living human being – living in your sense – who performs. No others but the great creative intelligences are able by the checking quality of their ideas actually to create on the physical plane. If we would effect an actual manifestation or clothing of any portion of reality in your sphere, we must not only work through the intermediation of one of yourselves, but we must do it indirectly, so to speak, by arousing you to make your own effort. We can direct you straightaway to do a certain thing, simply by telling you to do it; and you will do it and will apparently gain to a certain effect. But in the result will be no iota of the substance of reality, nor permanence; and in the inevitable readjustments it will be as if it had never been. Of what avail then to lead you on by direct advice? One blows down the wind! What you want, what the flow of progress wants, what we want, is rather the single grain of sand than the oceans of drifting fog.

"And I must repeat that the only mechanism we know to place this clothed reality in your world is the carnate human will."

— **2** —

This subject of the individual's part in creation was considered important enough for repeated discussion. On one occasion they devoted a whole evening to it.

"We will this night," they began, "consider the function of the individual. It is twofold: first as a channel, and second as an expression of the Universal. The first deals purely with his Being; the second, with his activities. It is of the first I would talk this evening.

"A channel, to be of the greatest use, must be as unobstructed as possible, as wide as possible and as strong as possible. Usefulness gauges on all these three. Without a free channel the flow is slowed and moiled. With a constructed channel the flow becomes betrickled. Without strength of channel the capacity must be reduced; for capacity is not mere containment, but the force of the flow that its walls will resist. The degree of use, therefore, depends directly upon the degree to which these three qualities are developed. By them is measured the caliber of the individual.

"A certain degree of them is natively inherent; but sufficient only for the mere preservation of personal spiritual life. A wider usefulness than that is then only incidental to almost accidental harmonies, or to harmonious manipulation from without. Only as *conscious* acquisition and affirmance establish these qualities, can the use of them be consciously bestowed. So the beginning of all our education is in emphasis upon personal unfoldment. Charity not only begins at home; it must begin at home!

"The importance of this matter resides in the basic fact that the only possible impingement of the spirit upon earth affairs must take place through earth creations. To adopt a figure of speech that is sufficiently awkward, but adequate for a picture: conceive your earth surrounded by an insulation impervious save through the perforations of these individual channels. Without them our essences of harmony, would have no ingress; and only through them are we able to bring to human affairs those influences we would bestow. Once entered, they may spread to their appointments; but enter they may not save through these channels, knowledgedly and toilfully prepared.

"The responsibility of the individual as a channel is self-evident. That particular responsibility is the keeping of his own integrity. That he has other responsibilities goes without saying, but we do not treat of them now. His duty in this connection is to keep his channel clear and free by the constant uprush of his spirit toward its Source. He must grow it wide. He must guard and keep its fabric whole and strong.

"What threatens that strength, and why is its integrity important? Because, just as the power of harmony and construction flows into its upper teachings, so may the powers of destruction and disharmony enter into it, but only through weaknesses or ruptures of its walls. It is as though, to continue our awkward figure, the channel from the Universal, before reaching earth, passed through a muck; and this, entering through crack or fissure, fogged and muddied and moiled and made dark and heavy the original purity. Were we to conceive all channels hard and intact, then only the clear purities would water the earth.

"The unclarified sediment that presses to enter we have various names for – such as hatred, avarice, egoistic power, cruelty and the like. These are active corrosives eating into the insulation, natural or consciously constructed, that guards the purity of the flow. Their eating through to the softening of danger has for each its recognizable complement in your consciousness. These also we name, but without clear, conscious pairing with its corrosive. Thus you say you feel irritated, angry, impatient, resentful, envious, fearful, without reflecting that these are really subjective symptoms of warnings reflexed from outside. They are to be attended as such; and taken as signals, like the ache of a tooth, that surfaces must be strengthened or breaches repaired. The apparent proximate cause is unimportant, nor must the apparent insignificance of mere vexation purchase indifference or condonings. A small softness, yielding, may expand to an inrush that can be stopped only by an effort robbed from usefulness. It is easy to dismiss, as of trivial importance, the habit, for example, of small moments of irritation. But each is a soft spot to which the irritation would call your attention of repair. One does not wrestle with the irritation itself, to subdue it saintly, for one wrestles to no purpose with an abstract thing. But one sounds the wall in search of the thinning that permitted the enemy tapping to reach and abrade your senses. This real cause is important, whether the symptom seems to be or not. He of superior intelligence heeds the whisper, where the lout must be aroused by shoutings. And since serenity is also a symptom, and not a primary, one does not strive to 'recapture his serenity,' but to establish that state whose atmosphere serenity is.[*]

---

[*] This concept of the "soft spot" is more fully treated in *Anchors to Windward*.

"Naturally, perfection in this process cannot obtain short of full and universal individual development. But the degree of the integrity of his channel is each man's task and responsibility. Construction of the self, viewed in this functioning, is the average man's foremost task in this stage of evolution. The arousing of awareness of the fact that this task faces them is the next step forward of the lower majority. The guarding of the complete wholeness of one's integrity in excluding the forces of disharmony is a not-to-be-forgotten importance for those who have accomplished conscious control.

"Clear: expand: strengthen: guard. That is the epitome of man as a channel of the divine."

— 3 —

In returning to this subject another time, the Invisibles warned of misinterpretation if we took their phrasing too literally.

"In what I say I must use figures of speech, and I would warn you to remember that they are not over-rigid containers of fact, but flexible illustrations of condition. You must never permit a figure of speech to harden.

"The conduit, from the Source through the individual to his environment, is composed of the spiritual integrity of the individual. In ideal it is strong enough and impervious enough to exclude completely deterrence or destruction; for the only entrance possible to them is through the walls of the channel, as it passes through these forces from the Source to transmuted application. I have told you the importance of small, what I call soft spots, as possible points of enlarging ingress for inharmonious forces. I have told you that these soft spots are products of corrosion from within incepted by the individual's own reactions. Now, it is obvious that such things as the larger hatreds, avarices, resentments, self-centerednesses and the like are dangerous weaknesses. But it is not so obvious that the small irritations may, if permitted to recur, often and unchecked, make pin points of perforation susceptible of perilous enlargement by pressure of forces inrushing toward the spot of yielding. That we have expressed before in other words.

"It may not, however, be so well understood that other attitudes of mind, especially if allowed to become habitual, may exercise a similar corrosive action on the channel's integrity. In everything with which we come in contact, in our incomplete stage of evolution, there is a minglement of perfection, of incompletion, and of the inharmonious. We may even fasten on one to the total exclusion of the others. There again is a matter of our choice. If we exclude the harmonious reaction, and concentrate on the incomplete and disharmonious aspect, we thereby distill as powerful a corrosive as would the undiluted destructiveness of pure maleficence. But, if we will focus on the harmonious element, however small in quantitative minority; and will ignore the rest, refusing to it a natural emotional reaction; we thereby become possessed of strengthening, instead of corrosive, material. Therefore, the habit of mind should be consciously and continuously cultivated, of selecting for reaction within one's self the constructive encouragement of the pleasant and agreeable element; and of refusing any reaction whatever, save the intellectual attention necessary to manage, to the fragmentary, the disagreeable and the angering."

— 4 —

So much for our job as "channels of the divine." Later on the Invisibles – and Betty – took up our "other aspect as active expressions of the divine." It is not enough for us just to build ourselves as channels – if such a thing were possible. Pleasurable fulfillment of function demands also that we do something about use of what we have built.

"We have talked of channels," observed Betty, "but we have not attempted to put the flow through them. We just constructed the idea of making ourselves channels, without any particular responsibility for filling those channels. That was supposed to come automatically, while we remained passive and merely kept the channel open. But now we must induce a flow."

Later on, when she had made further progress, she had this to say:

"I see myself as I used to be, convinced of the essential tuning process, without which we are nothing; doing it more or less regularly; luxuriating in it, even. But now that picture is repellent to me: it has no joyous dynamics. The prospect ahead is ever so much more satisfactory. Where before the picture was like a lake, now it is a flowing river. It would be impossible after this for me to return to the apathetic stage – except periodically for rest, or if I became conscious of nervous tensions, or for healing if ill. Now that I feel the stupendous stir of making a current by opening my outlets, no longer could I *abide* the self-containment of the still-pond-no-more-moving days!"

"It is the greatest of all sensations," agreed the Invisible, "this alignment with what might be called the Great Doing – this alignment of one's self with it, not merely to *feel*, passively, the flow, but to try out one's allotment of it, actively and enthusiastically.

"In fact, what *is* enthusiasm but this? What is energy but this? What is love itself but this? – this removal of barriers, enabling force to flow forward and back as necessity dictates: forward to accomplishment of law forms in matter; backward to recharge and refresh in the primal force."

— 5 —

This flow-through, to repeat, is our most important function in the scheme of things. Its conscious development must be our next great advance in evolution. But also we must be content to begin slowly and proceed carefully. Betty's experience showed this. In the beginning it dealt mostly with large generalities.

"I want to tell you," said she one time, "how you go about it when you are in contact with primal force out of which you are to make something – when you are in the reality of things, and not merely their completed detailed manifestations. The way I go about it is this:

"I know the life force we have been talking about is all that you've got to begin your work with. All you have is the amount you can take and arrange. I take stock of myself; sense how much current is around me which keeps at bay, as it were, what would be an all-engulfing substance if I'd let it. But I'm not going to let it: I'm going to act on it. That is as near as I can get to the sensation, the first primitive sensation of creative force which I manufacture and maintain.

"It is the growth of this sensation of greater and greater radius of superior force acting on the primal substance which will make it possible for me to establish my ideal, what I actually am capable of, what my *species* is in the universal plan. I said species because my ideal, my little atomic arrangement I am capable of making and arranging, establishes my species in the universe. And I am capable of changing it continually.

"This makes one's share in the whole universe dependent on the amount of the life force one is capable of generating and utilizing. One's individual participation in the abounding beauty of the whole Plan is dependent on the responsibility and coherence of one's own efforts."

"The point is," said the Invisible, "there exists in you, indefinitely developable, an engine of power capable of molding and impressing your material world according as you can give out from your inner being this creative force. This is not primarily the *mentally* creative force, which you understand perfectly. It is the higher sense of that mentally creative force, the vital principle of life. This I must touch on before I leave it: I must try to get it into words. The mentally creative principle is a mere ground plan. It has, by laborious process, to have its vital principle supplied. The true creative force, this godhead creative force, carries its vital principle with it. It comes not from the agent of the soul, the intellect; it comes from the very plexus of life, which contains everything in potentiality."

— 6 —

For most of us anything resembling the perfection of the creative process is hard even to imagine. We are told, but the words cannot register. Betty herself, when she first realized its possibilities, was wonder-struck.

"Such a big step!" she exclaimed. "Never to work alone. A deliberate hookup before every action: the accomplishment of that is the end and purpose of one's whole life. It is so simple and yet so tremendous – just like an electrical hookup.

"Before I start anything I must drop my consciousness into place as a link between the Purpose I do not understand, and the little act of which I am master. It is the definite awareness of this hookup and the practice of it that makes it work, lets in the power. It is just a workaday natural action – my two hands directed by my spirit. If that were an accomplished habit, there would be no necessity for wrong or puzzlement. I would just say to Unknown Purpose: 'I am ready when you are,' and keep a steady confidence in the purpose at hand; and in ripeness it would be done better than I could plan it."

"The entire secret," explained the Invisible, "is to make your hookup *every* time, before you get into action in minutiae and routines. There is nothing really new in this. The only clarification is the simple yet amazing thought that the law of empowerment depends on utilizing this hookup *for every separate act*."

XV Intention

Everything you see or touch or measure, or can become cognizant of by any imaginable means, is always the external manifestation of Intention.

INVISIBLE

IT'S LIKE a big pool of water: it's all there, but you have to dip out some of it in your own cup and use it – make it yours. Everybody is in this saturated pool of knowledge or power or whatever you want to call it, but it isn't any good to him unless he takes some of it out and INTENTIONS it.

INVISIBLE

— 1 —

THE positive element we, individually, consciously, are able to contribute to the creative process can best be understood by the word *intentioning*. The current of life is passing through us, in quantity and pressure according to our capacity to receive and conduct. It is an undifferentiated force. What specific form it is to take in manifestation depends entirely on our purpose and intention.

Our own understanding of the idea was begun by the discussion of Margaret's "currents" mentioned in Chapter XIII. She had discovered, you will recall, that she could induce between her hands what seemed to be various currents of force. The remarks by the Invisible here need restatement in part.

"It is all one force. It is a differentiation for

especial purposes of the one stream of vitality... It is evident only when arrested... Arrested by an *idea* it becomes a creature or thing... Slowed by a purpose it becomes a vehicle for differentiated force, dependent for its nature and effect on – the purpose."

"I have a friend," said Margaret at this point, "who seems to be able to perform cures at a distance. How do you explain that?"

"All results of this kind are gained by a slowing down of the universal vital current by intentioning. The use of the hands is not essential to this intentioning. Your hands are of help to you just as a broom is of help in cleaning – one can also blow down the dust. There are various methods of applying the force. Try them out."

"That would need some thought," said Margaret. "I am at a loss as to just how I should apply my efforts in expanding my work. Perhaps you could indicate the lines I should follow up."

"We do not know that exactly ourselves," confessed the Invisible. "The ways spread out like a fan before you, and yourself must to a great extent decide which to take. Remember all this is experiment for us as well. This is a pioneer work, and we cannot know the future in detail."

"Perhaps if you could give the differences between the three kinds of current it would be helpful," suggested someone.

"It is all the same force. Only the intentioning varies," repeated the Invisible.

"Is this intentioning done on your side?" asked Margaret.

"Some of it is done by us, but more and more is being done by you," was the answer. "I would suggest that in experimenting you note on paper the result of each current. By the gradual accumulation of facts in this way you will eventually come to see the underlying plan."

"What is the purpose of the cold current – or must I grow into that knowledge, too?" asked Margaret.

"Sometimes we use it merely to indicate our presence. Often its purpose – this again is a symbol, and not to be taken as a literal statement of fact – is to clear the path for the other currents: a cleaning of the conduits, so to speak." "Will it prove valuable to work with doctors on the subject?" asked another of us.

"Try. If they prove to be donkeys, we will turn them out to graze," replied the Invisible drily.

"Do you consider it necessary to prove a spiritistic connection with the currents?" came our next question.

"That is not important. What theories people have about it does not matter. They must simply be made to realize that this great vital principle is here to be used by anybody. The rest will develop later."

176

He indicated that he would like to try an experiment.

"Sit in an easy chair, Margaret." She obeyed. "Are you comfortable? Now let go; sink down. Deep down. And while you are deep down you will feel this current from above you, from where you were."

"On the contrary," objected Margaret after a few moments, "I seem myself to be about three feet above."

The Invisible chuckled. "It's a matter of definition," said he. "What is it that you call yourself? Leave your old self down. The current will then pass through you. It is the same current you pass to others. It is the healing current."

"I get the current all right. It's cool."

"Imagine to yourself," continued the Invisible, "that you continue to let it flow, but that you focus a part of it; through your hands, for instance. Simply deflect for a purpose a portion out through your hands."

"I feel it coming in, but it seems different when it goes out," said Margaret.

"You have done by yourself what we have done before," the Invisible congratulated. "This is the first lesson. We helped you only at the beginning by putting you in the current. The rest you did yourself. It is very good. This is only the first lesson."

A little later the Invisible continued:

"This is for Margaret, and is just a hint as to her participation in what she is doing. She must realize once again the importance of the substance of thought, and that the fashioning tool at her command is constructive imagination. I want very emphatically to get this conception out of the figurative and into the literal. It is an actual modeling tool on an actual, definite substance.

"Now no matter how imperfectly, how haltingly, or how intermittently she may succeed in fashioning the idea, always on applying these currents of hers she must go through this definite effort. Tonight we have partly disengaged her in order to assure for demonstration purposes a permeability to the greater current, greater than is possible at present and unassisted when she is in her normal consciousness. We expect her to use these currents in her normal consciousness; at first almost entirely by our own manipulation, later with lessening assistance, and finally, we hope, in practical independence.

"Whenever you apply this power, try to remember, and as far as possible duplicate, your impression of the greater current coming into you from above, sweeping through you as a fresh breeze blows. Imagine that picture. Always conceive of it. It will be difficult at first to gain any sense of reality, but not too difficult to obtain a fancy. One must begin small. Always do that. It fashions the conditions we desire in the substance of thought.

Then try once more to imagine deflecting a certain portion of this current to pass outward in focused form – not merely permitting the broad sweep, but focusing, as of water in a pipe."

After which, of course, the next step is determining exactly what kind of a focused current one is to produce; and that in turn is a matter of intentioning it. In this present case for healing.

– 2 –

In discussion it developed that a further distinction must be made between the intentioning of the general kind of current desired – as for healing – and the detailed application of it. The latter is also something to be determined and always by intelligence. On some occasions that intelligence can be our own conscious mind; on others we have not sufficient knowledge to understand what is good for the situation. Part of growing is the finding out which is which.

To take, again, the example of healing. We can intention the flow-through to become a healing current; but then we should turn over the job to other intelligence than our brain-mind. If we try to direct the healing process consciously and in detail, we may cause the patient more harm than good. In the next chapter we will take this up more fully. Meanwhile, the important thing is the general principle. *The most we can safely demand* is that the current intentioned for healing may be used for the best good of the one we would help. The question of what is his best good we must leave, in faith, to higher intelligence than our own reasoning faculties.

This need for caution seems to apply even to so general a beneficence as inspiration. One of us asked whether we should intention along the line of one's main purpose* whatever inspiration one may receive from the Source. The Invisible who was then talking to us replied that he did not believe in this sort of specialization; that putting things into separate compartments is always unwise; that so to intention might defeat the nourishment of subordinate purpose; that no one is wholly of one purpose, but is compacted of all the purposes; that ordinarily one functions most in the purpose to which one's temperament leads him; but consciously and intellectually to force one's intention to that purpose is apt to make one lopsided.

— **3** —

All this would seem to take things pretty much out of our hands. If we are to be safe, apparently, we must confine ourselves to large fuzzy Intentions with no comers on them. Everything else must be left to Higher Intelligence.

But such is not always the case. There are many fields in which we can intention to our hearts' content with little danger of stepping too hard on anyone's toes. One of the best of these includes all kinds of artistic creation. Here we can study how intentioning really works.

"Any manifestation whatever," said the Invisible, "is an effort of creative intelligence of one kind or another. The outward expression follows upon the inward creative fashioning. That inward creative fashioning, wherever exerted, in whatever form manifested, is always the same sort of thing: a tuning into the universal power, and a stepping down of that

---

* See *The Seven Purposes* for an explanation of this term.

power into a degree that will manifest.

"It is this principle which lies back of the creative power of thought – though that is to some extent a misnomer. The creative power of fashioning imagination would be better. Whatever is so fashioned must clothe itself – somewhere and somehow, now or later – in outward manifestation; simply because it has been given form and exists now where it did not exist before, like a mold, capacious to be filled when conditions supply the materials for that filling. In this sense, therefore, no genuine creative effort is ever lost. It has produced a phase of harmony which has not existed in exactly that form before. It has added to the harmonious differentiation of the universe detailed bits that have heretofore had no existence."

A definite and productive creation, then, has actually been accomplished even before the physical comes into visibility. The clearly formed Intention is a kind of intermediate step between original potentiality and objective manifestation.

"This fashioning dynamic creation," continued the Invisible, "of the opportunities for manifestation of potentiality is one function of the finite universe, and also of the slowly climbing intelligences which it originates and of which it is composed. As we see it now, the circle in whatever is the inunderstandable Purpose will be rounded out only when all potentiality is brought forth consciously and made evident. Furthermore, even the potentiality itself is the intelligent creative act of the Great Originator.

"There are two aspects to note in the wee corollary which each human will apply to himself. First, attention should be called to the fact that intelligence does not create harmony, but comes into attunement with harmony, which it can utilize only according to the power of its will to achieve. The second aspect is that no genuine creation is without result. A mold may be placed upon the shelf awaiting in due time the molten. But the shape exists in the universe, where existence it had not before. Nor will its eternal quality be limited by any small manifestations of form which may at one nine or another be made by its means. The mold remains intact for the uses of harmony at its need.

"I would say one other word, on behalf of the unrecognized. Creative genius is composed of two actions. These may conceivably be combined in one individual; or each may find its embodiment in a different individual. The conception of a thing must first be made in the substance of thought, and then precipitated in manifestation on your physical plane. This, as I say, may be combined in one individual, so that a man conceives his vision and embodies it.

"But not infrequently you have the spectacle of one who struggles frustrated throughout his life, without arrival at the world's success. You have on the other hand the spectacle of one producing abundantly and beautifully, almost as it were by instinct, without labor, almost without taking thought, a child of good fortune. One is condemned as a failure; the other is almost revered in his success. Nevertheless, often the first, the failure, has made true his vision; and the other, the genius, has done no more than possess the open eye wherewith to see, and the hand wherewith, unknowing to his own soul, to pass on.

"The measure of progress is not always the work

of the hand, but is often the inner fashioning."

— 4 —

Another time the Invisible strengthened the lines of this picture of Intention.

"You have had enunciated to you the principle that the precipitation or manifestation in the physical world, of any specific quality of consciousness at any one point in space, is because at that point have been gathered the conditions for that manifestation. The gathering of these conditions is intelligent, but works out through the orderliness of law. Man creates by assembling conditions for the working of the law. When conditions are assembled, the law must work. This is all old material, as you will recognize.

"It is possible for any given thing to be born into physical matter only when the Idea of that thing has been intelligently formulated. If a man would build a chair, he has first conceived of it in his mind. He has, next, consciousness of the different steps of the process of manufacture in his mind. He has worked out his chair complete in the substance of thought, so that an Intention exists, complete in all its details, into the mold of which, so to speak, a precipitation may take place.

"This is increasingly striking as one ascends into the creation of hitherto unknown forms of imaginative art. The creative imagination of the artist actually forms a mold for physical manifestation which has not heretofore existed. But more: he assembles conditions heretofore unassembled, so that always hereafter that particular mold is in existence and at the command of whoever in the future shall reattune himself to it in the substance of thought – which you call race memory, cosmic memory or universal memory – where nothing is lost. Thus it does not greatly matter if the product of his hands be destroyed. It yet remains in cosmos as a fulfilled potentiality which has not been fulfilled before. It exists in the substance of thought, and may at some future time be reprecipitated by one whose receptivity or sensitiveness attunes him thereto.

"Go farther. Consider the man who, from ineptness of mechanical aptitude, or from the frustration of ill luck or fate, or from the confinement of opportunity, fails in the production of that which his vision has seen and his imagination has molded. He has what you call failed. The work of his hands crumbles, the sound of his voice dies against a void of emptiness. He is alone, and frustrated and discountenanced and perhaps derided. Nevertheless, in the reality which I have called the substance of thought, he has had the genius and imagination to have made a pattern of gathered conditions heretofore non-existent. That thing he has visioned is in actual being. The notes of his music are imprisoned in a crystal stillness which needs but the touch for their releasement. The accomplishment of his spirit is in the cosmic Intention, awaiting embodiment, as definitely as are the cosmic Intentions of such old-established things as a tree or a dog or a flower or an ant or whatever. That Intention of his is rounded and whole, needing for physical expression merely the gathering of the appropriate conditions, as fire awaits but the knowledged placing of fuel and chemical action.

"I say this so you may know that any real or sincere creative effort is never lost. It is builded into the structure of the evolving universe. It carries onward into the way of progressing complexity as certainly as has the evolution of the bird from the reptile in the primordial slime. There are no failures, save those to carry forward wholeheartedly one's work and one's destiny as they reveal themselves.

"You have spoken this evening of one you described as in advance of his time – one who has called himself a failure. These things are incompatible one with another, for the man in advance of his time is not a failure. Nor can he write himself down as such, until the impetus of his vision and his desire has expended itself, and it has been borne in upon him that he has builded his vision in the cardboard of selfish desire rather than in the eternal substance of true aspiration. If the former, his effort will crumble unfulfilled. If the latter, its fulfillment – somehow, or through somebody – is eventually certain.

"It is in this thought that I would leave you, for it is a thought applicable to all endeavor. In it is the safeguard for all adventure. If one desires to build anew for the sake of visioning that which has not existed before; without thought of self-aggrandizement beyond what is a proper pride in function fulfilled; then one cannot go astray. Approach all work with a spirit of joyous fashioning, content to offer it upon the altar of the great Unseen, there to rest or to be handed back for employment as greater powers than yourselves deem wise."

XVI Healing

PAIN, suffering, all earth experiences are like the coloring used on the slides of a microscope to make you conscious of invisible things.

INVISIBLE

— 1 —

THE word "healing" really should be used here in a wider sense than the mere righting of bodily derangements. It should be made to mean also any effort toward restoration of harmony wherever harmony has been disturbed. However the technique of that restoration so closely follows, or parallels, the principles of bodily healing that first of all it will pay us to review what the Invisibles had to say to us on that.

In the first place, it seems all methods of healing, whether the sheer mental at one extreme and the drug system at the other, work basically on the same principle. "Sickness in your limited universe existence," said the Invisible, "is nothing but a maladjustment of frequency. Each entity has its own degree frequency." Treatment is the application of frequencies which will restore the normal adjustment. In mental healing, spiritual healing, some sorts of therapy such as the electrical, this is obvious when one stops to think of it, for frequencies are their obvious basis. But, said the Invisibles, drugs are merely another and indirect way of supplying the same thing. They set up in the body a chemical action which releases frequencies that stimulate frequency in higher degrees of consciousness. "Since all consciousness has the frequency of its own degree; and since each and every organ of the body has its individual frequency which makes it what it is, any method of such stimulation works in the same way and with the same results."

The method most appropriate to any specific case depends on the factors of that case – all the factors, mental, spiritual and physical. No man can say without knowing these factors which school of healing is going to work. Any of them may work provided they have basically the power to administer frequencies that will "take," so to speak. The purely mental and faith treatments will have no effect whatever on the skeptic; they will help greatly the one open to such frequencies.

Sometimes – indeed I am inclined to think most times – the matter is not so open and shut. In the future, people may not be so dogmatic and exclusive about their therapeutic beliefs. The medical doctor will not snort so loudly, nor the Christian Scientist recoil from occasional dosage with such horror. And the allopathic lion and the homeopathic lamb may lie down together.

The child of one of our friends had pneumonia. The parent was in a turmoil of anxiety whether he ought to depend on what were then his "faith healing" beliefs, or follow the allopathic or the homeopathic urgings of his various advisors. Betty reported back her consultation with a doctor in the Invisible. "He says to render unto Caesar the things that are Caesar's. He says that very gradually people are coming to realize that, especially in a somewhat developed personality, the body and the thing it clothes are more interdependent and homogeneous than is the case with those of less development. The latter may be treated entirely through the body for an illness of the body. With the former class, however, a combination is essential. One must render to the Body, Caesar, the best that is known in the treatment of the body. At the same time there should be corresponding treatment in the higher planes. He emphasizes that neither is properly effective without the other. The reason is the homogeneity."

But the parent tried to insist upon a decision.

"What does he think about light rays and homeopathy?" he asked Betty.

The Invisible doctor took over directly. He reiterated that the value depends on the circumstance. "But on purely theoretical grounds homeopathy overemphasizes what might be called astral effects and underemphasizes material effects. *unintelligently* applied allopathic medicine does the reverse. Whatever his expressed theory, the homeopath is depending more on the 'astral' chemistry than on the effect of his little pills. As to the lights: they are a physical thing. Properly administered they are a therapeutic thing. The use solely of the spiritual currents is open to the same objection, in lesser degree, as homeopathy – as I first pointed out. In a person of wholly undeveloped homogeneity – if such were conceivable – your spiritual currents would act only indirectly and dilutedly. In a more developed homogeneity the effect would be more direct. However, supplemented by their physical counterparts that effect would be more easily and completely attained. That is self-evident, is it not? Though you might be capable of swimming ashore, why not use an available boat?

"It is an equally absurd negation, of course, to concentrate upon the purely physical chemical reaction in the case of a highly organized individual."

"I cannot see, then," said our friend, "why there should be a conflict between the two medical schools."

"Allopathy is as near an absolute as your present knowledge can produce on the physical plane; whereas homeopathy is far from an absolute of what could be accomplished on the astral plane by other and more intelligent methods. Homeopathy imagines it is acting on the physical plane, but is a dabbler in both. It is a mixture. Study to combine the methods most effective in each. Why use only one crutch when you have two?"

As for complete reliance in all circumstances on the power of mind or faith, one of us finally summed up the discussion this way:

"These people have gone off on a tangent. Their lack is that they do not recognize the lower degrees of frequency that are designed to affect the frequencies of the human frame. Actually, there are drugs, also, adapted to change crossed frequencies and reduced frequencies. You should use both mental AND physical treatment. It is just as foolish to deny one as the other. There is such a thing as tapping the Source, and the Christian Scientist has put all the weight there. But he denies all the physical things put in the world to be used for healing, in addition to tapping the Source. After all, the modern healer – whether a medical doctor or not – is utilizing light and heat and electricity and all sorts of frequencies, in addition to his drugs. A while ago they depended entirely on drugs."

And recurring to the same topic on another and much later occasion, the Invisible had this to say, apropos of a specific case:

"With your present concept and understanding of frequency and its relation to absolute time and space, I think you could, after a few times, open your mind to the inflow for restoring the depleted frequency of your body. You SHOULD use your mind. That is one of the truths that has made Christian Science live. The difficulty there is that, having added the unlimited universe healing properties to the earth concept, they immediately eliminated the degree frequencies of drugs. Now both should be used. If a tool is at hand, why disdain it, if it can aid you? What is needed in this particular case is a very fine nerve healing, and there just happens to be no immediate drug that will do the trick. You say, 'Time will do it.' Well, what does that mean? Nothing but an accumulation period for the sick nerve; because the only thing the matter with the nerve is its own depleted frequency. When you understand illness and pain from this angle, you can see why the Christian Scientist's healer, not through the laying on of hands, but through the deliberate opening of the mind, does get results."

"The Christian Science faith has a great deal of truth in it," – this was Betty, from the unobstructed – "as you know, it is a great glimpse."

— **2** —

We must not get the false impression that any of

these schools of healing or of medicine were mentioned by the Invisibles in any but an illustrative way – certainly in no critical spirit. Rather the effort seemed to be to establish a denominator common to all of them, and at the same time to show that no one of them is complete in itself. Two things are basic, no matter what the system.

(a) There is an observable effect on the physical body.

(b) The application requires especial knowledge and training.

Those propositions are self-evident in medical science. Drugs and surgery do things to our bodies; and most certainly it is reasonable to trust their administration only to a qualified physician.

The self-evidence also obtains as respects the effects of mind, or spirit, or faith on the body, but not to the same degree. We are likely to be more vague as to that. Everybody knows that when we are ashamed, or angry, we turn red; when we are frightened, we turn pale; when we are swept by any too-violent emotion, our stomachs go back on us. Shame, anger, emotion are purely mental and subjective; the flush or draining of blood in the cheeks, and the gastric spasms are purely physical. These are phenomena so common that we give them no thought. Their significance was impressed on me when, nearly fifty years ago, in Paris, I saw Charcot hypnotize a woman, inform her that he was about to drop sulphuric acid on her hand, and then in fact did use water from his laboratory tap. The water could have had no such drastic effect as the acid. *Nevertheless, in a few moments dull red spots appeared!*

Now there was a definite physical effect induced by a mental image. It did not differ from the flush on the cheek; but it was certainly more striking. And if pure unaided idea can bring blood to the face or form stigmata on the hands, it is reasonable that properly directed and strong enough ideas are capable of doing things to the body that might be of some use. No one could mend broken bones that way, but one can help bruised flesh. Try it next time you drop anything heavy and painful on your foot. What do we usually do when that happens to us? We raise the foot off the floor, and scrooch up all our toes, and concentrate our enraged feelings into a *tension* of the whole member. The result is a violent contraction, which blocks every blood passage in the afflicted part, denying entrance to the very fluid which alone is capable of both carrying away damaged tissues and bringing fresh material for repair. As an experiment, try consciously to do the opposite. Relax the foot, allowing it to "spread out," devoid of all tension, as flat on the floor as possible. Instead of thinking how much it hurts, and so inducing the contraction that accompanies pain, concentrate your mind on a picture of the injured member opened, so to speak, by this conscious relaxation to an accelerated flow of blood through it; and focus attention on an image of this accelerated flow. What you are after is a sort of consciously self-induced blush to the foot, if that does not sound too fantastic. You will be surprised at two things. In the first place there will be nowhere near so much pain, and in the second place there will not be nearly as severe a bruise. There is nothing obscure or occult about it. You have merely given nature a chance to get in where the trouble is; instead of blocking her out by nerve-contracted muscles until it is too late. It works: I've done it many times.

— 3 —

All this is simple and elementary, and will seem too much so to many. But we are supposed to go on from there. Our job is to extend the application of the principle. We do not have to "let nature take its course." Often we can do something about it.

"Let us assume a simple illustration that you can readily understand," said the Invisible. "To laugh and to cry are physical acts. Do you know that when the emotions are not so deep as to be beyond control, under ordinary circumstances when you start to cry, if you screw your face muscles into the physical formation of laughter, you can laugh? It is also possible to apply the power of will controlling the physical acts to readjust mental states. Take, for an example, the ordinary emotion of fear. Many a man who has been afraid has eventually overcome his cowardice by a physical simulation of bravery. This may be carried to the nth power and can be made to control even more delicate and less understandable emotions." Another time the Invisible applied the principle to actual self-treatment for illness.

"Now take the case of a person," said he, "who feels himself threatened by a common cold. The misapprehension of the principle I would elucidate advises in one breath a denial of the existence of the cold, and in the next breath a positive assertion that the individual is perfectly all right and that nothing whatever is the matter. Sometimes these are used in conjunction; sometimes they represent quite different schools of therapeutics. Both are an affront to common sense. The cold *does* exist, and the individual is not in a perfectly normal condition. No matter how vehemently this point may be asseverated by the conscious will, it must arouse a reverberation of denial from that subconscious element which is in touch with truth. This denial is in itself a suggestion stronger and more effective than the original voluntarily pumped-up assertion. Therefore, the latter end of this experiment is complete failure. Instead of bearing aid to the threatened boundaries, you have acted the part of a clamant pacifist remaining safely at home in an illusory security.

"The first process of healing from the psycho centers must consist in an acknowledgment, definitely formulated, of the state of affairs. You say to the body politic of your complicated physical structure: 'Yes, you are invaded. Germs have obtained a foothold in our territory. It is necessary to assemble the fighting units of the white corpuscles to overcome and eject the intruders in the usual and proper manner.' This is a statement of simple, acceptable fact, and arouses no harmful suggestion of denial. The cells and processes in question receive no wrong impulse which will confuse them in what is actually their accustomed and proper work.

"In many cases, unaided, they might be able to accomplish the task, but you must do more. Still looking upon yourself as the center, the animating over-source, through whom vitality must filter from even a higher source to the cells, you must project to them a confidence that they will be able to do the job: 'To be sure we are invaded, but we will down them, put them out – that is foregone.' Thus have established you in your capitol a party of serene confidence, in place of the usual panic-stricken defeatists. Do not you see that in the one case you have a pressure outwards, and in the other case you have a vacuum which sucks in?

194

"That feeling of confidence and outward serenity is often again sufficient, but it is not the whole. To continue our figure, you must further say: 'Something is wrong; we must fight; I know you can do it; I have confidence – but I will also send you aid. I will not merely stand aside from the great flow of vital consciousness that fills and makes all cosmos; I will consciously attract to myself a greater allowance than customary to flow through me in assistance at this emergency.' You *purpose* this, and that purpose – in itself a real thing in the substance of thought, mind you – slows down, checks, offers a resistance to, and differentiates into a certain kind, a portion of the universal flow of vitality, and sends it through you in the direction appointed.

"Then, having done this, without tension, without strain, easily, naturally, you go about your business and forget it."

The last statement was later explained to refer to one's ordinary *mental* processes. It did not mean to go about physical occupations regardless. One's place might welt be in bed. The main thing is not to brood on one's condition.

"If," continued the Invisible, "you hold the thought of cold constantly in your mind, some little devil will pass it through your lines in spite of your good soldiers. Only when you feel a scrape of the throat, a wee bit sneeze, some little shiver – then you know your soldiers send you a message: 'We are beleaguered. Brace up!' But if you do not get such a message, forget it.

"This is much pother about a common cold, is it

not? I use such care because it is the simplest possible example of the working of the law."

"How about cancer and smallpox and such virulent diseases?" we asked. "Can they too be cured by this method?"

"Sometimes, of course," acknowledged the Invisible, "your soldiers are overcome by a superior force, and then you will have a devastated area, so to speak. Yet if you use this method you will have a lighter smallpox."

"I understand the idea," said one of us doubtfully, "but I am pretty unsuccessful at putting it into practice."

"The probability is," said the Invisible, "that you make too particular an application. I gave an example of self-healing method with a common cold. The moment a particularized attention attempts to direct healing power toward a specific thing, you may help – or you may energize the ailment. You may be furnishing vitality to the disease. The thing that takes, appropriates, is not under your command. You must leave to your physical headquarters the use of what you supply, according to its own wisdom. It is the direct application that is harmful. You can never apply power direct, either to yourself, to your friend, or to the world.

"While remembering this, however, do not forget that still you must direct the abundance you take for yourself – deliver it, so to speak, at the door of your physical headquarters, and not just leave it scattered about."

"Couldn't one give help to someone about to be operated on by directing this sort of 'general help' toward the surgeon – not in specific detail, but in aiding to steadiness, or sharpening his skill, and so on?"

It sounded like a good suggestion, but the Invisible was doubtful.

"You cannot tell, in impinging on a human being like a surgeon, what cross currents you are introducing into a situation already balanced. You may safely offer a *situation* all the harmony you can produce, because if a situation is balanced, all its component parts must be.

"That is why this whole subject has been held in abeyance, because too often harm comes not only to the patient, but to those attempting to help. We do not encourage the uninstructed to experiment in this dangerous field."

"How about the very aged?" persisted our questioner. "Cannot you send help either to preserve life or to help in passing? Isn't that desirable?"

"Desirable, perhaps, but not with the specific intention to bring about either life or passing. Your wish is to send him, of your abundance, *that thing which he needs*, whether that be life, or death, or increased vitality, or the subduing of his forces to ease the launching. That is legitimate. It is the specific intentioning that bums and destroys when you would help."

— **4** —

On another occasion a different Invisible summed up our present status as regards the attempting of detailed ministration.

"It is an immensely complex subject; and in it are grave dangers of harming the very one you want to help. A misplaced intensity of the limited mind is so easily substituted for intensity of the heart, which knows the higher laws. Then you particularize merely your own desires and limited perceptions, and so restrict the very person you wish to free. It becomes an impertinence, a spiritual impertinence, *as is any restriction of freedom.*

"A fostering by sending forth harmonious influences from the heart batteries is quite another thing. That reaches corresponding life principles in the patient and unfolds them naturally for him. The use of projective mentality to help him by means of your own selection of positives and negatives is always a risk; but it can be attempted with reasonable safety when projected in the vehicle of affection. It then has no sustained power to restrict.

"This subject is tremendous. Only through years of experiment and practice can its laws be proved. It is the entire next grade of life – the technique of the spiritual functions."[*]

---

[*] This whole principle has been pointed up even more sharply in what we came to call the "Tommy-tonsillitis" case. It is get down in *Anchors to Windward*, pages 86-88.

— 5 —

There remains but one aspect to discuss, that of "nerves." What can we do about that?

"So-called 'control of nerves' is an important item," acknowledged the Invisible, "for the mere sake of personal comfort, if nothing else. You do not, however, control your nerves. They act – and they report – on stimulus. If the stimulus is physical, you call it real. Example: the physical commotion of an indigestible green apple. If the stimulus is emotional, you speak of nervous reflex. Example: the total inhibition of digestion by a shock of grief or fear. The stimulus may also be habit or memory – yes, nerves have memory. Example: discomfort without any assignable cause *at the moment*. All these stimuli impinge first on your subconscious, as that part of you directly in charge of automatic bodily function, and are then by it brought to your conscious mind for attention.

"You 'control' the first two – the physical stimuli – by removal of the cause, if that is possible. Otherwise you pay the price of indiscretion or accident, applying whatever of palliative or remedy is at your command. But you cannot prevent the reports coming in to you as long as there is reason for them. The same may be said for the second class of stimulus.

"The third are different. You cannot get the better of them merely by ignoring them. The reports may be based on unreality, but those reports themselves are real. However, you can, and should, prevent those reports from reaching your conscious mind. You can do so by imposing on the subconscious a duty of discrimination. The subconscious should be made to feel, by your attitude toward it, that part of its business is to sift out the actual and to inhibit the small baseless panics; to understand that you are not going to tolerate its running to you with its unsifted unimportances. Just as you would frown upon a child's always running to you with every little problem. It is the province of the subconscious to superintend the memory-habits of the physical nerves, which are its direct charge. This discrimination is within the power of the subconscious, and it can be trained to exercise it.

"Of course, in the larger sense, the subconscious is not actually a separate entity, though we are apparently treating it as such. But for the purpose of function it can be made so, *just as you are a separate entity for the functioning purpose of the whole, with which nevertheless you are actually integral.*

"It is a mistake to 'control your nerves' directly through your conscious mind, ignoring the mechanism in whose charge they are."

XVII The Area of Accomplishment

Disharmony is nothing eternal, for the reason that it is merely incompletion. And incompletion cannot exist for a longer time than it takes for some creative intelligence to tune in upon, and bring to manifestation, the complementing vibration.

INVISIBLE

THE whole universe is a mutual back-and-forth helping and building, each assisting the other's completion, but at the same time completing as well as he can his own.

INVISIBLE

— 1 —

THE material in the preceding chapter was only incidentally intended to instruct us in healing ourselves or others. Rather it was so directed merely because such healing most clearly exemplifies the basic principles underlying help to others of whatever kind. The Invisibles themselves stated this specifically.

"We deal not so much with the narrow aspect of healing as with the technique of helping," said they.

"The basic principle is that one can most effectively help another, and with concomitant benefit to one's self, only in one way: that is *through the bestowal of abundance, transmitted by personality into individual contribution*. That compact sentence should be well studied, for it contains the whole matter.

"The first step, then, is to assure an intake of abundance to be passed through the personality for transmutation. As the occasion may be assumed to be one of emergency beyond the normal, it follows that, if possible, the flow through the personality may be with advantage accelerated beyond the usual. That is because, naturally, outgiving cannot exceed intaking – except for a brief period – without ending in depletion. Furthermore, as accelerated flow can be maintained only by continuous attention, the major effort must *continue* to be concentrated on that assurance of abundance for one's self. Whatever there is of minor technique – in intentioning, directing and applying – must be subordinate, and done with the left of the eye, so to speak."

There, once more, is the "charity begins at home" insistence.

"That statement," continued the Invisible, "deals with only one phase – abundance."

Abundance of what? The life force, the flow from the Source? Not exactly. The basic principle quoted above adds a significant modifier: "transmuted by personality into individual contribution." If we are really to help anyone, in healing or otherwise, there must be a transmutation.

"It is," warned the Invisible, "harmful to attempt a short cut, to try to invoke, inundate your subject with, pure power from the Source. That cannot be your contribution. So understand these two things: that your contribution must be from your own abundance; and that you cannot meddle with your subject's own functioning in pure power, force, vitality, life, spiritual abundance."

Now the final consideration, which ties us into the principles of healing: here, also, we should give only a *general* directive to the overflow of abundance we contribute.

"The idea is," said the Invisible, "that it is unwise to focus application on the details of a specific trouble. In trying to help someone, all you should do is to determine in intention that you desire your abundance be accepted by the one you would help. The seat of his trouble may not be where you think, and the proper application of your abundance may well be elsewhere. Perhaps, also, its best influence on the trouble may be indirect, through a further transformation by the subject himself. You have not the wisdom to determine that. Even when the difficulty appears to be as sharply defined as a belly-ache from unripened fruit, you should be chary of applying a spiritual posset to the affected part. Be assured that, if you turn your force in the proper direction, and allow it – not force it – to seek its application, you have done your part. An attempt to focus it into a beam may burn too deep."

Not, admitted the Invisible, that such a method may not sometimes work. It does. In many instances. "But if so, it is in spite of."

"Is it," asked one of us, "a good idea to try to help people in this way, if they need it, whether they ask for it or know about it or not?"

The Invisible did not care to commit himself categorically as to that. Too many modifying circumstances. However:

"One may state broadly that a psychic intrusion is as discourteous as a physical intrusion. Speaking very generally it is not a desirable procedure. There are exceptions. This is not a dogma."

— 2 —

One discourse by the Invisibles on the subject of psychic help is so revealing that I will quote it verbatim. First, however, I will epitomize to break trail.

Every man – so runs the treatise – has a certain spiritual caliber which determines three things:

His obligation to attempt spiritual help. How far it extends.

His safety in doing so. How far he can go without danger.

The field he can work in with reasonable expectation of results.

These three, according to the Invisible, represent a certain area of responsibility wherein he can move with confidence that he is not overstepping his privilege or his powers. Any job he is to tackle he must draw into this safe area. If the job is not meant for him, he will not be able to do so. Then, if he is to meddle with it at all, he will be forced to go outside his area – and there lies danger and futility. As in everything else, however, a policy of isolationism is not the idea. There is sometimes justification for exploration, or even for the sortie of a forlorn hope.

All of which is admittedly in the region of what the Invisibles called the "ultra violet of inspiration," and so out of our workaday vision. But it is also what the Invisibles called a "fructifying glimpse," which in due time bears its harvest in our consciousness if we attend it seriously. As to practice, however – here, now, today – it is a bit vague. We must have something definite to do. Just exactly how are we to draw a given job to us?

The secret is again in the word "love." If we feel that toward the job – and just to the extent that we do feel it – the job is brought into our area of accomplishment. The way to increase this ingredient, as we have seen, is to establish contact with the Source. Once we have freed our channel in this way, the normal reaction is an eagerness to use it for service. That is, of course, right and proper, but it exposes us to two dangers.

One is the temptation, once the flow is established, to hurry it through the channel to its application. Such a procedure forgets the charity-begins-at-home aspect we have so often had emphasized – the nourishment of the person himself.

The second danger is that the eagerness for service may tempt beyond one's proper area of accomplishment. Ambition for service, however, is not dampened when one discovers that the capacity of his area is not determined by its extent, but by his power of attraction through love.

There we have the essentials. Now we will let the Invisible take over.

"The flow of vital and spiritual force received by the individual from the Source is according to the capacity of his attainment. It passes through him, as it were, and spreads about him in an area corresponding to his conductivity. In one of low development this area extends but little beyond his own shadow. As be evolves, it becomes larger. But at any stage it defines at once his area of responsibility; his area of possible safety; and his area of possible comfortable and efficient accomplishment. It is, as it were, the radiation of his spiritual transforming.

"Those things which he draws into this area are his for manipulation. In his bestowal of his transmutations of the spiritual, his method is not to cast out beyond the luminous area of his own radiation, but to attract within it the objects or the persons of his concern. That he may venture beyond, in service or hope of service, is acknowledged. And in emergency at times it may even be justified. But such venturing is with grave danger of disaster, defeat, or at least failure.

"As an example of proper function: if one desires to bring help or health to a friend, he does not project out to that friend, but brings the friend into his own assured attainment. If he would contemplate the accomplishment of a labor, he does not decide whether it is possible to reach out to its doing, but whether it is possible completely to transport that task into his area or radiation.

"This drawing inward cannot be done by taking thought. The only force for this transportation is that of an interest so wholehearted and sympathetic that it will generate a magnetism of attraction. One draws inward to one's self, and therefore into one's beneficent influence, by means of one power only; that of loving to the point of appropriation. This is a statement in reverse of what has been told you: that one should give only from overflow. It is another way of saying that spiritually, as well as otherwise, one must work within his capacity, comfortably, without strain. This, viewed from the spiritual side, is normally the sure, effective, and safe way for the individual to function.

"Emergency may require a temporary increase of pressure beyond normal capacity. It may require outward venturing from the radiance into darkness. But the emergency must always be declared by the heart and not the head; and that call should be listened for in silence, and with the perceptions opened toward the Source.

"Eagerness for service, once the channel to the Source is freed, too often leads to two neglects. The one hurries through the stream of vital spirit without permitting it to perform its first and necessary nourishment of the person himself. That must always be first attended to, for without it the channel becomes brittle and will break. If no more flows in than suffices for this, then for this it should be employed. Only when the spiritual tissues are moistened and made flexible may that which remains, and that which shall come, be released to its natural seepage outward.

"The second neglect is in not restraining one's desire to one's own proper area of accomplishment. Ambition for service is not thereby abridged, when one discovers that the containing capacity of that area is not limited by its extent, but only by one's power of loving attraction. In the least accomplishment may be room for a universe, if the heart be large enough.

"So I give you, in simplest form, stripped of many modifying details, the outline plan of ideal indi-vidual action on things outside your own constitution. This plan will be found beneath all modifications. The mind-directed action, by which purpose is actively manifested in deeds and fashionings, is a matter to do with the brain after the heart has laid the deep founda-tions."

XVIII The Place of the Intellect

THE first thing for you to do is to stop looking at things too closely with your mental vision. The second is to put all your energy into looking at them as wide landscapes. Then, third, you must put in the foreground of the little things of your world the friends and the passing of cheerful days. The instruction will come if you follow this plan, and will come when you are furthest away from trying to make it all out. We can only instruct when you have a relaxed mind, and not one full of your own puzzles. This is so tremendously important with you that I am tempted to say it over and over. I can reach you best when you are not trying so hard to understand it all, but are simply occupied with some commonplace thing. How can I bring to your conscious mind, your controlling motor force, the knowledge and wisdom you want? If you could once get into your head the conviction that you keep deliberately shutting the door in my face when you tie yourself all up in hard thinking knots!

INVISIBLE

— 1 —

THE last sentence of the preceding chapter points the way to the next problem in the creative process: the proper use of the intellect in shaping the final product. This subject has been so completely explored in the other books that further treatment here would be redundant. Nevertheless, its importance is such at this stage of our present argument that it must be briefly restated.

One of the great modem difficulties in the way of human advancement, the Invisibles maintained, is the premature use of the intellect in fields to which it is unadapted, and for purposes for which it is not intended. It is a valuable tool, they acknowledged, but it is only a tool.

"Heaven forbid," cried one of them, "that I should decry the human brain, but it should be proportioned. The eternal self must be developed as a fit controlling power. In trying to act *directly* on the highest – call it organ – possessed by man, his eternal spirit, we are constantly interfered with by the more developed side of him, which clamors, *insists* on translating every instinct into its own language, and limiting it to his own experience and comprehension."[*]

In The Road I Know, my own comment on the Invisibles' attitude I expressed as follows:

"For a long time they *seemed* to have almost a contempt for the intellect. That proved not to be really so. Merely, for the moment, the intellect was not the appropriate tool... The whole thing boiled down to one simple statement: the brain is the executive, not the originating branch of our personal government."[†]

— **2** —

We nevertheless have so long depended principally on our "reasoning powers" as the only solid basis for actions, that we have raised it on a pedestal as

---

[*] From *The Betty Book*. This whole interview, pages 65-69, is worth reading.

[†] Again I recommend reading the whole argument as set down in *The Road I Know*, Chapter X.

the boss, whereas it is merely a useful subordinate. The testimony of many – and of my own personal experience for that matter – is to the effect that final solutions to problems, first clues to inventions, most of the highest ideas we later elaborate, are not logically built structures but flashes of insight. The pride of intellect has confused us as to its actual placement in our personal cosmos.

The distinction was most clearly brought out for us in connection with a narrower subject. We were discussing Joan's method of communication; asking Betty how she, in the unobstructed, went about it.

"Well," said she to Darby, "suppose you tell me what you do when you want to say a sentence, and get it to Stewart."

"Why," said Darby, "I suppose I set up a frequency – of sound – which impinges itself on Stewart's mechanism, and he – perhaps unconsciously – transforms it to an impression on his mind. I suppose you work in an analogous way, only you don't use sound."

"Go back further," said Betty.

"Can't," objected Darby. "I don't know what my mind is, only certain results from it. I produce certain effects, but I don't know how I do it."

"Well," proposed Betty, "let's take it backwards. You said that a spoken sentence by you is carried by Stewart's auditory nerves to his brain. The auditory nerves of the ear carry to the auditory centers of his brain the impingement of your spoken sentence, picked up from your mind and translated to your consciousness. Thus we have got this sentence into Stewart's mind, by way of his brain. It has been a successive impingement of varying frequencies. Now the method of communication I use is such a succession. There is first my desire to communicate with you. That is my I-am wish. The desire sets my mind in motion. I start it working with this idea. You have a mechanism of vocal cords and such equipment, an entity of frequency which you control and operate, somewhat subconsciously. I have in parallel all the essential organs. So I must have something that resembles your brain."

"Go on!" jeered Darby. "You are utterly brainless!"

Betty usually rose to this sort of thing with relish. But now she remained serious.

"All right," she rejoined with dignity, "call it energized will then. Communication through this station approximates the operation by which you got your idea to Stewart. It is the voluntary submergence of the station's I-am, and then the impingement by me on this mind of my energized will. But then it has to go through her *brain*, and that is when you get your coloring."

"In other words," Darby pursued the argument, "that brain acts as a transformer. All frequencies are of a piece, though differing in degree. What the brain does is to pick up the auditory sensation and transform that frequency into another type of frequency, which ultimately spells my idea to his mind. That, then, is

Joan's brain function? Her brain is able to transform the type of frequency you manipulate just as mine does the frequency of the vocal cords. Is that it?"

Here is where Betty underscored the distinction.

"I do not manipulate her brain. I impinge on her *mind*. That is my point: I want you to distinguish between them."

When we consider that the intellect, in its operation, is actually a brain-child, the significance of the distinction will be plain. Betty was here really trying to explain communication. Skipping for the moment the specifically technical, Betty had this further to offer on the present interest.

"Suppose I were to say that the mind is the operative faculty of the brain... So I intensify my own frequency to control the frequency of Joan's mind, and she translates that over to her brain."

Betty here used a term which needs explaining: "form attribute." The external, material body – of whatever variety of consciousness – is the form attribute of that consciousness. My body is the form attribute of the habitual consciousness which is myself. The tree we have in our front yard is the form attribute of that quality of consciousness which represents "treeness".

"Never forget," said Betty, "the universal importance of trilogy. In this case it is I-am, mind, brain. The brain is the actual material, dissectible, form

213

attribute: the mind you have not yet drawn pictures of. Or the I-am either – only its form attribute. The body in the obstructed universe is the form attribute of the individual I-am. The brain in the obstructed universe is the form attribute of the individual I-am mind. Think about that."

— 3 —

The following passage is worth quoting – aside from the beauty of its style – as throwing quite good indirect lighting on the subject. It was from an Invisible who, as was usual, refused to name himself. Betty called him Tangent because of his indirect darting method of attacking a subject. He sometimes referred to himself as the Teller of Tales.

"Words as you know them," he began, "are always following limpingly behind the winged thing they would express and which they can never overtake. They can but fix glimpses, shadows. The thing they can sit down to examine is already a shell from which life has all but flown. That is why an expression in words is always lacking in the vital principle; why it fixes merely a thing that has ceased to move. An idea that is living always moves, and can itself be embodied only in a thing that is similarly fluid.

"The language one must speak in telling of the higher and spiritual essentials is made up, not of words, but of those moving, ever-changing things known as actions. We have often told you in one way or another that the mere intellectual formulation is nothing. It expresses nothing, and in final analysis it conveys nothing of value to the only true auditor of the deeper human life which is man's real speech. It is because of this truth that we have in times past, bunglingly and *in petto* [in the breast], urged you to 'make it so,' and have urged you to act more on impulse. Impulsive action is the instantaneous and directest expression of that which, *when unperverted by false habit,* comes to you from primal sources. It is then undiluted by passage through the fixed and stationary medium of words by which reflective wisdom formulates. One might almost say that the language we who are advanced into a more liberated spiritual medium hear from your side is the language, not of this reflective deliberation, but of your actions.

"Action is the language we speak and understand; a fluid, flowing language, ever-changing, ever moving in company with that which it expresses. That is why we look, not to formulated belief for our encouragement of progress, but to the moving force within, which causes a man to do or to refrain from that which comes to his hands. The one is an arrestation, a fixing perhaps of a dead thing, while the living thing wings its way out of sight; the other is an expression of what that man perceives, though he may not intellectually know. In the ultimate freeing from a mechanism temporarily useful there comes a time when this language of action is the natural method of expression and communication between entities; when one does not say 'I love,' but loves; when movement follows rhythm beautifully; when the *construction* of thought – which, you must remember, is a reality – is a joyous fashioning:'

He paused. Then after a few moments went on:

"But I am warned to go no further in this, as it can but give a fragmentary and false impression. The

215

very word 'action' is itself too heavy-footed to follow this subtle, flexible and delicate reality. 'As a man thinks, so he does' is not so true as that as he does, so will he eventually think, when leaden-footed thought has overtaken."

— 4 —

However, in spite of that disclaimer, Tangent did pick up the subject again at a later session.

"There are," he began unexpectedly, "two examples under your eyes of instant translation into action of direct impulse: a flock of birds in evolution, and a school of fish. You have often seen a dense mass of such birds as sandpipers or pigeons wheeling, turning, changing direction in close formation, with all the speed and precision of a perfect drill. The hesitation of a tenth of a second by any single member must inevitably throw the whole into jostling confusion. There is manifestly no room for the communication of an idea through any medium of expression, no matter how simple or instantaneous, through a mechanism such as a brain. The expression must of itself be the action. It is not a question of receiving an impulse and deciding to act on it; nor of receiving an Impulse and diverting it into the groove of even long-established habit. It is, to repeat, necessarily the accompanying external manifestation, in direct expression, of the impulse.

"What the impulse signifies in bird life is not the question here. It is sufficient to say that it is not without its meaning; that the apparently aimless rapid twinklings through space are, not too fancifully, phrases of the directer language of which we lately spoke. The illustration is mentioned, not as an important thesis,

216

but as an enriching corollary to our former talk.

"Impulsive action in the case of the human entity in earth life must not be confused with the following of whim. Whim is merely the product of capricious desire. It should not be too difficult to distinguish that which wells up spontaneously out of the inner being, from that which merely flashes across the surface, illuminating perhaps a desirable possibility.

"At first it may be almost impossible to obtain that flexibility of spirit which will receive accurately and undistorted the real impulse from the depths of being – the impulse which will translate itself into the sure action that is its expression. One stammers and hesitates and uses wrong words and awkward phrases in attempting any new or little-accustomed language. One who tries blindly to follow impulse in action will make many blunders and mistakes. This will occur for two reasons: first, because of the distortion or perversion of habit of thought or doubt of experience; and, second, because the first and pure impulse is not brought to conscious attention before it has been diluted. Thought, for all its mechanical nature, is extraordinarily swift, and fairly before the flash of perception has reached the consciousness it may unconsciously interpose a hundred considerations that modify it. What we think is the pure impulse has thus become a hybrid before it reaches its expression in action. Only with practice and with mistake can fluency and accuracy in this language, as in all others, be obtained. But this should not discourage the attempt.

"Let this consideration hearten you: If you will review the decisions, and the results of those decisions, to which you have come by painful intellectual process, and which you have weighed and measured and balanced and considered; you will – if you are honest – be forced to admit that the proportion of mistakes has been as great and as disastrous and as little shot through with success, as could possibly attend even the blind following of all you might suspect to be impulse."

Possibly Tangent felt he might have been overenthusiastic, for his next words were a warning.

"But do not lose sight of the fact that the intellect is indeed a useful tool. With it, in its analytical aspect, you are enabled after the fact to analyze and parse the construction, so to speak, of the expression you have made in the directer language. Not to question its wisdom or unwisdom, but to search back unflinchingly to the original naked impulse which you have clothed in the expression of action. Determine, if you can, whether that expression has been a true one, whether you have actually followed the real first impulse, or a perversion or dilution; and try to see if in actual fact an accurate following in action of the real first impulse would not have placed you in the path of wisdom. By this means, little by little your command both of your perception and your ability in accurate expression will grow.

"It is almost: impossible to introduce through this inflexible medium all the modifying and explanatory qualities necessary to a satisfactorily complete exposition. I must call your attention briefly to the fact that the intellect has its undisputed field of activity in that which concerns it. It is a physical thing, and it is created to deal with physical things. It would be absurd to 'act on impulse' in the common acceptation of the term when dealing with the correlations and vagaries of physical crises. Experience plus reason must guide you through conscious intellectual thinking. Solve the difficulty with the tool that is adapted to it. But in dealing with affairs that you may loosely designate as moral or spiritual, which includes your relations with yourself, with your fellow beings and with the greater unities, then the tool you must use, the language you must speak, in order to be understood where you must be understood, is the direct expression of which we have told.

"This is very fragmentary, open to many doubts and questionings. It is necessarily so because of the fact that it is translated from that identical flexible closely corresponding language into an alien tongue. As one should turn Shakespeare into Chinook. But the central idea is there; and being entertained, even if not completely understood, must force its own expression in its own proper tongue."

— **5** —

Still another Invisible, on still another occasion, summed it all up.

"Machinery lying idle rusts. Only use keeps it efficient. Machinery does not move without the application of power which is not integral with itself. Knowledge is machinery; wisdom is power. Power is not generated by machinery. Wisdom is not generated by knowledge. Power is not dependent on machinery. The usefulness of machinery is wholly dependent on power. Power's directed application is dependent on machinery. The understanding of the machine, intellectually and consciously, always does take place at some time or another. This time may be before the period of the machine's greatest usefulness; it may be at the time; or it may be after the machine has practically subserved its purpose. In the first case it produces instinctive action; in the second, purely reasoned action; and in the third, provides a basis for action of another sort in a step forward in development. In all three cases the 'make it so' element is fully carried out. As to which type is used in any one case depends either on the individual's temperament or make-up, or on the kind of action, or on the function in development that action is to fulfill.

"This, in itself – what I have described – is a mechanism. Therefore, Whether it also is to act through intellect, instinctively or intuitively, depends on those elements."

XIX Law

Self-managed individuality; self-directed intention; freedom through obedience; liberty through fellowship: of such is the Law.

INVISIBLE

REMEMBER always that the Law smiles for those who sit serene in the midst of it; for it is their Friend.

INVISIBLE

— 1 —

WE DECIDED at the very start that ultimate Purpose was beyond our grasp, but that a twofold immediate objective could be recognized. One aspect, that of individual self-development, we then traced through the more or less automatic stage of blind instinctive progress, to the threshold of conscious spiritual participation. From there we set out on an investigation of the methods and techniques suited to this new field.

During these explorations we have repeatedly crossed the trail of the second aspect of the universal Aim: the evolution of a functioning Unity. In fact, once we had arrived at conscious spiritual contact, we found this aim implied in practically every move we were called upon to make. Contact itself is an aspect of unity, and the purposes to which it can legitimately be put are of the same nature: communion, creation, healing, "help" in general.

All law, of whatever kind, is another aspect of unity. Those subject to the same laws are thereby and to that extent unified, whether they realize it or not. And this is true of man-made and natural laws alike. The former are a powerful binder for groups: cities, states, nations. The latter constitute a bond which ties all created things. And this bond carries over even into the invisible world.

– 2 –

Many years ago, through Joan in Our Unseen Guest, "Stephen" stressed what he then called parallel laws. By that he meant simply that every law we have here governing the processes of our earth is found in parallel in the invisible. This concept was sufficient for the purpose he then had in hand, and expressed truth, but the expression was only partial.

The definition sufficed until comparatively recently, when Betty, from the unobstructed, carried it further. It is not that there are parallel laws in the two aspects of the universe, said she. There is but one law. The reason its manifestation on earth may differ radically from its action in the invisible – when it does – is that the same law is working in different media.

The idea should not be wholly strange to us, for we can see the same thing even in our own physical environment. Electricity's laws, for instance, remain unaltered whether the result is heat, light or power. The difference is not in the laws but in the mechanism or medium through which they express themselves.

"Speaking of parallel law," said Betty – from the unobstructed, remember – "it's actually an extension of your law, that's all. If we are going to use the word parallel, we must make it clear that it is not two laws. Our laws, which we have termed parallels, are in reality an extension from the obstructed universe to the unobstructed universe of the same law. Or rather vice versa. What you call natural law is a reflection back of the absolute law governing my unlimited universe – and the entire universe. However, there are many laws operating in the entire universe that you have not yet discovered. When they are all discovered, it will indeed be all one universe. I can't tell you about them, for there are no words yet. There is a whole field still to be developed.

"Much as I dislike mathematics, yet the fact is these things are all mathematical and could be best explained by mathematics. The deeper we go into the thing, the simpler it becomes, because, as I told you, there is only one law. All you need do is to take your limited law and project it out into an unlimited operation. What understanding of limited law I brought with me has made it possible for me to adjust myself quickly and project myself into the understanding of, and cooperation with, the unlimited aspect of the same law. You must stress *extension*. Reach out along the limited laws you best understand, to meet me."

In the discussion which followed, the subject came up of positive and negative laws, constructive and destructive. Another Invisible had this to say:

"The Law is neutral; the Law acts. And it matters not whether it acts through the destruction of a great typhoon, or whether the same law blesses the fields of grain. Law is Law. Intelligence offers the conditions through which the Law must work. The Law works good

223

or evil according as the intention of the Intelligence is good or evil. The Law is in itself a duality, based upon its inherent unity. It will work one way with positive conditions, and diametrically the opposite way with negative conditions; so that ordinarily you say you have two laws... There is but one."

More discussion followed, during which one of us objected to the word "law."

"I think," he observed, "that the use of the word 'law' should be guarded. Our tendency is to regard law as an imposition from without, and the laws of consciousness are not imposed from without, but are inherent. I suggest the word 'principle'."

"I am glad you brought that up," said Betty, "but to me, and those working with me here, it seems that 'law' is properly chosen because it connotes a strength and compactness that 'principle' does not."

"I think there should be at least one clear statement explaining that laws, in this sense, are not impositions," persisted our objector.

"Yes," Betty agreed. "They are the *invariables* of consciousness. No man can change them; and he who breaks the law retards himself; and consciousness as a whole. But first himself; then his degree; then consciousness as a whole."

— 3 —

The end of this discussion was interesting because it underscored a conclusion arrived at nearly thirty years before, while Betty was still here.

"How do you distinguish," we were then asking, "between what you might call the laws of nature and the law-ordinances of a city? Seems to me they are quite different things."

"Let's look at them a minute," said the Invisible. "You've been told very clearly that nothing can happen except in accordance with law. That is true; keep that as your strong point. How would this do for a definition of law: Law is the fundamental design of things?"

"I don't exactly like that word design," objected our questioner, "because that means something preconceived."

"You can't get away from that, even when you can't understand the ultimate design," the Invisible assured him.

"You have to assume something that can rightly be called design, ultimate intention. Perhaps it will suit your mind better to substitute the words ultimate intention.

"Now let us go very carefully, because this isn't quite clear to you yet. Let us start with this tentative definition.

"Mathematics is the basic description of the inevitable interplay of anything. As somebody said to you, mathematics is the science of inevitable consequences. That is the bottom thing. Next, I should think, logic is the name that is given by men to the mathematics of the interplay of thinking. It is the science that has to do with the way the entity's substance you call thought-units of it – influence each other: it is the science of the interplay of thought. Chemistry is the science of the interplay of ultimate units of the substance you call matter. You can't make any real distinction any more between chemistry and physics, because the subject matter as you see it has become virtually the same; but you can make a distinction for practical purposes, because the units with which physics deals as a whole are, for your point of view, larger. Astronomy is only an extension of chemistry and physics. Chemistry deals with what you can discover standing in the midst of physics looking in; and astronomy is what you can discover standing in the midst of physics looking out. This is an arbitrary distinction, however; quite temporary, I assure you. Biology is the science that has to do with the units that have acquired what you arbitrarily call life, within which you have made a distinction, also arbitrary, between vegetable and animal. And so on. I think you can fit philosophy and religion and art and music and literature into their places in this arrangement by the application of mathematics.

"Go back to our original definition of law, as the statement of the Ultimate Intention. It is given to Intelligence, in any stage, to arrange the conditions under which the law will operate. The sequence of events, the interplay due to the arrangement, will take place automatically. Remember that, for it is the whole business.

226

"Now, out of his experience and memory of the way in which that-which-is-not-himself affects him, the individual entity adjusts his customs – his laws. But at times he attempts to do things that are not really in accordance with his experience and memory – he gets unduly exuberant. He can't disobey the Law – it can't be done – so he gets what he orders. To put it in theological terminology: God doesn't condemn him to hell; he *orders* hell – arranges the conditions for what you call hell. The process that follows is automatic; and you might even say that God himself couldn't prevent a fellow from getting hell, if that is what he orders.

"That's the basic fact of Justice. Things ARE equal or unequal; and if an equation is not satisfied, there is a vacuum – which is the one thing the Ultimate Intelligence can't stand for. Then the thing happens that's got to happen. That's justice. You can take any definition of Justice you can find, and if you take the cover off you'll see that it's just Cosmic Satisfaction; things hooked up right; the equation satisfied.

"This sense of the word, and understanding of the thing, is universal; and it is what has come to be called everywhere by the various kinds of names that mean Law. It's the bottom thing on which you stand, and have got to stand.

"Now men of all sorts and stages of development keep trying to adjust themselves to this. They build up customs, which in the last analysis are their ways of getting along comfortably with the Rest-of-Things; and the Rest-of-Things, mind you, includes EACH OTHER. These customs – sometimes temporary, in temporary situations or relationships, and sometimes what they call permanent – get written down or handed on: they are what you call 'laws.' But whether they are big or little, they are all attempts to arrange conditions so that the Law, the Ultimate Intention, shall work comfortably for them. Sometimes these laws are very lofty and unselfish in their conceptions, and represent a great wisdom – which is only another name for tried experience. Sometimes a little knot will succeed by one means or another in enforcing a set of conditions – or 'laws' – in which the Law will contribute temporarily to *their* comfort at the expense of wisdom. But either way, man-made laws are all measures for the arrangement of conditions in a search for the way to get along comfortably with the Rest-of-things. Calling a statement of this sort of thing a 'Law' doesn't make it either cosmically right or wise, but at the bottom it is the same attempt. Sometimes, of course, this attempt is premature."

"What about the obligation to observe these laws if we think they are 'premature'?" asked our practical member.

"Why, you can answer that yourself. You have to do what you think is right; just fix your mind on that. If you have the slightest compunction about wearing a red necktie, and still wear it, you have off ended against your own sense of right. It doesn't make any difference what anybody else may think about red neckties, or how red neckties may measure up against the Ultimate Intention, so far as others are concerned – you think it's wrong. And even if that thought lasts only a minute, if you then wear a red necktie you have by the exercise of your free will made a bad choice.

"As to evasion, or attempts at evasion, of the least of the laws, it all depends on you. If you think it's wrong, it's wrong for you, and you mustn't do it. You shut out Cosmic Satisfaction from your own self *by just that much.* This thing works in minute fractions of an ampere. It doesn't make any difference whether your mathematics errs by a hair's breadth or a mile. It is a very nice business – this thing of justice.

"Happiness is Cosmic Satisfaction, and Cosmic Satisfaction is happiness. The greatest joy you ever had, to the top of your capacity, was no greater *in quality* than the joy of the tack that popped over to a magnet. When anything happens *right*, that's joy; joy is the emotion that goes with that.

"So the test always comes in whether a law – a statute-made law – is inside of yourself. If in the light of the best wisdom you've got, you obey a law unwise in itself, you have the same effects within yourself that you would have gotten from obeying a good one.

"Of course there will often arise the necessity for a compromised attitude. In addition to your responsibility to yourself, there is the social group to be considered. The man who runs amuck with his own idea may be quite right in reference to himself, but all wrong in the light of the group. There is a sense in which obedience to a law you think not wise or right may contribute to a larger spirit of cooperation. So you can sometimes afford to abide by a bad decision on the part of others, if you do it saying, 'What's the odds? These are good fellows and they mean all right'"

— **4** —

The following day another Invisible seemed to feel that something should be added. We had been having a discussion as to the merit of doing disagreeable things "for the greater good."

"There is something more about the Law," said the Invisible. "The baby's confidence that the floor will hold hi is no accident. All this thought about the Law must be on the foundation of utter confidence in the Stability of Things. It is all right – the baby knows that with a knowledge that nothing could disturb. Even as the Law moves serenely on, or stands serenely founded – whichever way you want to put it – so the soul may stand serene amid the illusion of turmoil, sure that all is well.

"What we have told you in many ways, and on apparently diverse subjects, all has this for its foundation. *things* cannot go wrong. The only wrongness, or sense of turmoil, is within yourself. The only thing the Law cannot do is deprive you of your authority to command your own life; and by the same token, of your responsibility for your choice. More than that, with the same sureness each choice conditions in some measure the choice beyond. Somehow get, for yourself, and give to those upon whom you may have any influence, something of this serenity. I would say go to your contacts of any kind with joy, and try to make joyful those to which you are compelled, as it seems; though the fact that you are compelled to a joyless contact may well be your indication that the contact is not good, for you.

"I have in mind your discussion about doing things and taking attitudes apparently unloving, with intent to do some greater good. I cannot suggest any way by which you can evade the duty of choice at such points of contact, but I can warn you that the ground is boggy there. See to it that your choice is an honest one. There is always a great temptation to camouflage one's real motive, even to himself, in the guise of 'greater good.' Each time, from hour to hour, the choice must be your own and for your own good. Really, I think one may say that there is never any real doubt about what to do *right now*. The doubt is almost always about what you will do tomorrow. But no one ever has to decide tomorrow. The decisions are all made Now. There is no such thing as tomorrow. The serene confidence in the Law belongs to Now.

"So, the Law is not an abstraction that one may evade. The Law – any law, even a police regulation – exists only in the decision that you are making at any Now. And the judgment has to be your own. For at the base of Ultimate intention is self-determination."

XX De Senectute

I THINK the end of some people's lives is so pathetic, the period when they store their furniture and sit in an empty house.

BETTY

— 1 —

ONE of the amazing phenomena of life is that years succeed one another inexorably, and that in due time enough of them have gone by so that, unrealizing, we reach what is called "old age." Another amazement is that old age is not in the least like our preconceptions nor what we have been told about it. The preconceptions have been drawn from our mere observation of the alien class of human we called our elders. What we have been told about it is merely preconception of others, from no different a viewpoint than our own. We imagine, and we are told, what old age ought to be like, considering its outside circumstances. And from our present, and younger, vantage point it does not look attractive.

The only difficulty is that all this is ex parte [one-sided]. Those who have actually entered the later years do not bother to talk about them. It is not worth while to buck strong preconceptions. And anyway the matter is not important.

But this thing they do know, that the mere accumulation of years brings one into no different class of human, whether named as elders or otherwise. For no one ever feels old. He may feel handicapped by bodily restrictions, but he himself, the fellow inside him, does not recognize he is any different.

How one takes this somewhat dismaying contradiction depends on what he has learned in life. Not much of course – nobody seems to learn very much – but whether he has discovered something useful in orientations. For instance, the graceful and normal shift of importances. He who clings tenaciously to the importances of active years despairs when the physical equipment is not up to it. He who comes to realize after all that his body merely carries his intelligence to where he wishes to apply it, and that if it is adequate for that it will do, is in the way of useful contentment. As to the application of the intelligence, there too he is to apply a necessary shift of importance according to the wisdom life has brought him. He does not deny to the old significance its necessity. It is a mistake to think that. The accomplishment is still just as important as ever in and for its own sake. But not for his sake personally. In that balance he finds he can retain his former zests and his old interests in them, but without the pressure of urgency. His legs will no longer take him to the mountain top, but that does not matter because he has quite sufficiently been to many mountain tops, and he is not interested in more repetitions.

To some people the successive abandonments of what have been real and valued interests are appalling evidence of deprivation. We youngsters pity that state of mind. That is because we judge by our own present standards – how would we feel right now, if we were in that fix? There are some oldsters who feel that way, too! I think, however, that the normal majority ripen into new activities and standards and importances that bring satisfaction. They rarely say anything about it. In the first place they do not hope to be understood. In the second place it is not desirable that they be understood by those yet in journey. Any more than you youngsters are understanding me now.

— **2** —

I am led to that last remark because I know by our own experience that it is true. Many many years ago, when I was still climbing Alaskan mountains whistling, and scrambling up Alaskan rivers, and blithely penetrating remotenesses in Central Africa, the Invisibles told us things about "old age." They were sensible things, and we accepted them as graceful and picturesque statements of a charming thesis. Only latterly, now that I am embarked on my seventy-fourth year, do I find that the Invisibles meant them, literally, and that they work. I am now going to set down those things, merely to put them on record, to be discerned in rounded reality only when one gets to them. So they will be recognized when one does get to them. Together with my own endorsement that I find them genuine.

A certain repetition of what has been already published in some of the other books will be necessary.

First of all, the Invisibles refused to take seriously what we dread as drab and decrepit old age. We look on it that way because, said they, we insist on upholding a tradition, and allowing our attention to be deflected from the new territory we shall enter.

"You must never let your outer self, the physical deterioration, attract your attention. That is the trouble. As you grow older, you stop *looking* at things. That is old age.

And Betty herself, later, repeated the same thought.

"Old age!" she scorned. "But why old age at all? Old age is when you stop looking at things."

Or, if we do look, we look backward to our former capacities. There is no question that they have diminished. But how about our new capacities? It rarely occurs to us to look for them.

"We have come a long way from primitive man – in some respects. But not in others. Many of the old cave-days standards linger as sort of vestigial remains. Without realizing it, many of us pay disproportionate tribute to the capacities of the body. We are holding fast to the idea of physical energy as a symbol of the pinnacle of life. In a kind of arrested development we stick at the same point as the Neanderthal man, glorying in his belly exuberances... One of our illuminations at this time (i.e., the later years) is the recognition of the youth cult as a Neanderthal superstition."

For those beyond the half-way mark who have felt this drag of the backward glance, the Invisibles had a certain gentle derision.

"Imagine," said they, "an acorn just *devastated* with grief because it had cracked its shell in putting forth its first sprout toward being an oak tree! *its* onward-pressing conviction, maintaining the movement of life, leaves no regret for the fulfilled natural processes. Likewise with yourselves, mere accustomedness and sentiment must not retard and weaken the force of continuity. Youth welcomes every change; so should age! Age with imagination, age with freedom to forevision, unhampered by the metamorphosis of a completing cycle!

"Such an outlook is not too difficult, provided you use a little understanding. Consider the bright ardor of living, the fervid desires that you have in youth. They are possible principally because of the flexibility of the physical mechanism. The secret of this golden age is the freedom from bodily restraints. The leap of the flame is the natural process. In later years you strive to recapture this faculty. But, though the ideals you envision have now more substance than ever before, you cannot levitate and vitalize them. Every effort to do so merely stiffens and exhausts the body machine.

"The trouble is that you are trying to translate the ardor and fervor of the intangible substance of thought into terms of bodily tensions. That is a very great mistake. If you are going to face a great and shining future, you must use a new and bright apparatus with which to express your greater capacities. You can't think bright and shining thoughts with a tired old brain. So step aside from it, admitting that it is perhaps a little of everything you say. Why shouldn't it be, and what of it? It is only a protective covering now for the thing that counts, which is what generates your bright and shining thoughts – the new consciousness born within you.

"It is a sort of replacement idea. Once you grasp it clearly you will find you have within you a fountain of eternal youth. But it must be done *honestly*. You cannot come into possession of it if you hang onto old crowbait ideas of leaning on a stick and being weighty. The instant you find yourself leaning heavily on the waning powers of the body, snatch yourself away from it. Actually, it is a clumsy, moldy, wasteful idea; and the replacement idea is the truth. After all, why saturate your whole being with a sensation that has to do with only a smaller part of it? Even when the body is tired, there is no longer any need for you to live in its tiredness just take the sensible measures appropriate to a tired body, and then withdraw into your higher serenities.

"Of course, it would be silly to deny that you have lost what the college boys possess. But it would be equally silly for you to think in terms of this merely physical desirability, for you are engaged in growing something younger and better than they have. This thing you are ripening toward is the fruit of your life. It will make you bright inside, no matter what you are outside. It is a *shining* thing."

"We must teach ourselves to recognize it," Betty contributed. "It is there, awaiting our recognition, for our enjoyment and development. It is the fruit of consciousness which the college boys haven't got. As soon as we let drop from it the tired flesh-thoughts, we'll see how beautiful and buoyant and wonderful it is. But as long as we allow those old flesh-thoughts to sit around like old black crows, just spoiling the party, we'll never be able to believe in the fruit of our life. It will be obscured by the age of our arteries, denied by the stiffness of our muscles and every other old kill-joy in our bodies...

"The gift of illumination of the moment," resumed the Invisibles, "is how to substitute for bodily functions the higher intelligence and vital intensities of the enduring being within you. Age, in a sense, is self-inflicted, a legacy from past generations. But within each there is something that is superior to age. Once you fully realize this, there will be no tradition of age to uphold. It will exist only as a physical cycle, quite apart from the real center of being.

"And with this realization will come another: that you are not on the down slope toward bankruptcy of youth's qualities when youth itself is over – that there is something even better to look forward to: something with increasing instead of diminishing interest, and not merely limited to itself, but with vistas far into the future."

In the same line of thought, conversing with one of her Invisible friends, Betty reported this:

"It's hard for me to understand what she says. It's about the ripening of life. She says the fruition of life is tremendously beautiful if only it is understood and looked at. She is showing me so many things with that idea in it, but nobody is helping me with words.

"It is, roughly speaking, about what we miss by keeping the greenness of youth as a standard instead of the natural fulfillment of life which matures like a seed pod and renews itself. The seed-renewal idea is really younger than the greenness of youth, if it is merely the vitality of newness we want,"

"It is very important," said the Invisible, "to keep

your mind fastened to this; to the youth and health and strength of your inner self. That is your opportunity here and now, in spite of your handicaps and scars. You have within you a perfect new-born thing always to work on. You can begin yourself all over under the protection of your old shell. It is like a rebirth, here and now, of yourself. You cannot help the old bodily rubbish – which you may, or may not, have spoiled – but you can take the best of it, – and by walking surefootedly with all the strength you have, and giving as bountifully and as healthfully and eagerly, you will have a new self under your control. Always think of it as absolutely beautiful and young. Anything is possible to it. It is a new-born thing to live in and work on and enjoy. Don't be afraid to play with it."

You see, was the further gist, this procession of years is toward a ripening of something in us, just as the procession of days across spring and summer is a ripening. So why should we carry the idea in dread as a burden?

"This thing you are ripening toward, this fruit of your life, is something you do not rest heavily on in thinking about. It is rather something buoyant. You must teach yourself to recognize that. It is there awaiting your recognition, for your enjoyment and development.

"No amount of mere philosophizing will do it. It must be a lifting spirit, the thing itself. Happiness consists in lifting one's self up. Go back in thought to youth. Go back to where you began to drop it and let it sag and sag. Now pick it up and put it on your head with a swing, and start out again with it balanced – and your thoughts ahead, not on it. Your head must stay up and your shoulders must stay back to balance it. Now!

"Don't you ever think about the weight of years. It's all balanced: now go ahead!

"Blood is meant to circulate. An abundance of big forward ideas makes it circulate and tingle as reciprocally as exercise clears the brain. Go straight back to youth and pick it up where you dropped it. Go straight back to those incidents of life when you were in equilibrium, and live them over until you've freed yourself. That's the ripening of youth. It is in control. Rightly distributed, years cannot weigh, unless admitted to sensation. This admittance may be refused; must be. No exceptions, no treachery of mind secretly making concessions to the weight. It must be wholeheartedly, irrevocably established. Watch out for your own treachery. The explorations of the years supply the elements which compose ripening. It is too terrible to see people dragging their years, like refugees from life. Got to go away back, away back to where you put them down.

"You see what a pity it is not to make age as attractive as the ripening of youth? Such a pity to make age ugly!"

"Old age, or middle age," the Invisible amplified at another time, "is a too-heavy sensing of discipline, an accepting of its limitations as a wall and not as a channel in which we can ran as vigorously as ever. When we are slowed down or headed off in our former directions, we should just concentrate ourselves on the direction we can go in, with a greater outlook and insight. Successful maturity is a conservation of youth; the not spending of it profligately and recklessly as we used to, but a conserving and surety of use of it."

It is not easy, we never said it was, admitted the Invisible.

"The trouble is," said be, "this higher education is a progressive education, and since we and our forebears have not been trained to it we do not think that way. And I want to tell you right now, it is a very stupid thing not to try to get it. It makes you bright inside, no matter what you are outside."

The outside, he acknowledged, is going to deteriorate and become less useful as a machine. But, said he, "it would be silly not to accept one's age processes in a lightly held, humorous fashion. They are so unimportant if you can live youthfully in the psychic processes."

Being still ourselves comparatively young when the subject was first talked about, we had some reservations. The Invisible was just a little impatient.

"Now there's no question about it," he rejoined. "There's no use your saying it can't be done, because it can! Age is self-inflicted; self-inflicted by generations. There is something within each that is superior to age. If continuity of life is established there will be no etiquette – no tradition of age to uphold. It will exist only as a physical cycle apart from the real center of being."

As for the body itself, that takes some management. It is an entity with its expectations and

241

habits built from its experience of the kind of existence it has known.

"You have a new way of working, a dependence on mental and spiritual vigor, rather than physical, which is not possible in physical youth. It is a period of rare enjoyment – once you manage to overleap the largely magnified physical dictates; once you learn how wisely to manage the body; once you learn not to arouse its combative simulations, but to give it case and consideration. Even to pamper it excessively in order to gain its cooperation. See if you cannot transfer the vigor and abandon of youth, its enthusiasm for adventure, into the mental and spiritual integration you have acquired. In extreme cases invalids have acquired this technique and had exceptional adventures. Paradoxically, deference to the body is now the only way to overcome it! Thus cajoled it will serve you efficiently to the end."

XXI The Gentle Art of Dying

THERE is nothing supernatural about it – just advanced natural.

INVISIBLE

THE dogged heaviness of the person who has no beliefs and who acts solely from distaste for disintegration.

BETTY

— 1 —

OUR customary attitude toward what is told us about old age is, as outlined in the last chapter, one of intellectual approval but subconscious distrust. Only when we ourselves actually get there may we discover that it was not pretty rhetoric or pious conformity. We are able to find that out, if we live long enough and do not indulge in a deliberate arrested development.

It seems reasonable that the same might be said as to death. From all sorts of sources, in church and out of it, we are assured that there is really nothing to it; that there is nothing to dread; that we shall like it when we get to it. In my early childhood I had a nursemaid who tried to persuade me to spinach or castor oil or reasonable facsimiles thereof by solemnly assuring me that they would "taste just like ice cream." This I believed up to an actual experiment. Thereafter I looked upon her as a liar by the clock, and all her subsequent suggestions as suspect. The average human, deep down inside himself – nothing to do with his formal "beliefs" – has an inherited racial instinct that distrusts any and all things that taste just like ice cream. He would like to see somebody else try it first. The only difficulty in this particular case is that when somebody else does try it, he goes away permanently without stopping to make a report on whether it does or does not taste like ice cream.

We are dealing here with the mill-run of mankind. The testimony of the small minority who have actually received, or believe they have received, such reports makes little impression on the racial instinct of skepticism. Nevertheless, the news sent back is that, in general, what has been told to us turns out to be true. Like old age, no matter how forbidding it looks from a distance, or how undesirable in logic considered from where we sit right now, it will turn out to be as felicitous as any other phase of existence, once we actually get there. Below the racial instinct of skepticism there is, I think, a still deeper rock-bottom perception that this is so. For, if one analyzes it down, men do not dread death. What they dread is the dying.

This can be proved any day by a glance at the newspapers – that men do not fear death itself, I mean. From war to the simplest wayside rescue, men – not heroes, just plain ordinary men – unhesitatingly make what is known as the "supreme sacrifice." That is to say, they do so if the case is open and shut and they have no time to think of the possible maiming, pain, hospitals, crippling that may lie in wait on the way out. So as to the more usual procedure in merely growing old and passing out, we dread the approach of the close of life, not because it is the close, but because we fear it will be preceded by the disabilities and helplessness of senility. I think, if we could dig down to the secret thoughts of those on the threshold of those final years we would find there a sense of congratulation, perhaps of envy, whenever a contemporary is taken suddenly, without warning.

That the black-looking barrier across old age is not as formidable as it appears from a distance we have discussed in the chapter before this. We have had the testimony of certain of those who should know about it, the dwellers themselves of those later years. But the general feeling is that we have no such first-hand information as to death. Nobody, says the average man, has ever come back to tell us about it. And, he would add, if someone did I wouldn't believe it.

— 2 —

Well, of course, the latter part of that statement cannot be argued. But the first part is debatable. There have been reported and attested many experiences where men have died physically, according to the best medical tests, and have revived to tell about it. The interesting part of that is that they all say much the same things. As to one matter they are unanimous. The process is painless, comfortable, pleasurable. This testimony is unvarying whether the returned one "died" from disease or accident. These witnesses are here. One can talk to them face to face. And nobody can deny that it is they who are talking nor that they are the ones who apparently "died." The doctor can corroborate that.

— 3 —

There are other witnesses who say the same thing, with the elaborations of wider and further experience in the subject. They are the ones who did not revive back into our kind of life. We call them the Invisibles. What have these people to report? Quite a bit; both in theory and in practice, as one might say.

Perhaps it might be a good start if I were to set down the verbatim accounts of the very few who, for one reason or another, have seen fit to tell us how it seemed to them to die. Ordinarily the Invisibles appear not to bother with that type of curiosity. Once in a while, if we urged our interest strongly enough, someone might oblige. Occasionally a newcomer seemed to be so full of wonder over the unexpectedness that he would talk. These latter had the value of fresh impressions. Anyway, here are a few.

The first was a young fellow, a great friend of ours, killed in an automobile accident.

"It was all a breathless crash of a hurry with a long-drawn quavery kind of bewilderment. There isn't much joy and rapture at first when you come so hurriedly and have no one eager for you. You know how it is in learning any new stunt: it seldom seems as good as the old ones you can do; but there was such a tremendous impulse in me to try to understand that I soon won out; and now it is so much more wonderful and interesting all the time, I would go through anything to et here. I long to spill over telling you about it. In the first place, it is the real intellectual freedom I always dreamed of, mixed with something else that inspires and satisfies and expands as intellectual pursuits never actually do, when you line them up alongside a man building a fence, for instance. That is the difference here I note the most, the proportion to everything, nothing lopsided or unbalanced."

"Who first met you there?" we asked.

"I don't know exactly myself. So much just seemed to seep into me, as if I had sprung a leak somewhere. I didn't have any one person taking me gently by the hand. All I can say is, in the Bible term, I was just plain ministered unto."

The next was a woman of middle age who brushed aside as unimportant the actual fact of dying to talk of her reaction to her new estate.

"In the first place we are just as interested in the novelty of our surroundings as you were when you first found yourself in Africa. I have a keen delight in everything and am as full of questions as a child. Think of the most alive and intensely exciting moment of your life and make it a whole day or a week and you will know how I feel over here."

By way of variety here is a man, a great friend of ours, who had never given a moment's thought, as far as we knew, to any of these matters. His death took place only after a painful illness. It is to that he refers in the first two sentences.

"I didn't like it much. It was darned uncomfortable, for I suffered a lot and could not be sure of myself for some time. Now I cannot imagine why I did not understand what was going on and why I made such a fuss about it. I came to without any pain and did not believe it; but that was enough for me just at first. I wanted to keep still and feel well. Then I got so full of pep I ran around in circles. My body didn't interest me much. I did not hang around it, for I think I passed out and went to sleep at first. I saw a man I used to know in the old days. He hung around to be sociable and it helped, for at best you feet like a cat in a strange garret except that it's all so exciting."

Now for a simple soul, a colored woman, one of those lifelong retainers in Betty's family, loved by them all.

"The first person I saw," she answered Betty's question, "was my dear lady, Mrs. Calvert, and my brothers and several others. I was so pleased to see them I was just tickled to death. I thought I was dreaming and would not believe them when they told me. I think I rested some time, for I did not feel a bit tired or sick in my head any more. I am having a grand time, and everybody is so good to me, showing me around and explaining things."

And the last I shall quote from these new immigrants, rather than old inhabitants, of the new land, was an artist. He had died only a short time before, perhaps too recently to permit of direct communication, and it was Betty reporting.

"A beautiful pattern of transition," said she. "There is nothing to dying. Just a tickly sensation; that's all. So natural; so real. I am with F., but there is no desire to talk yet. He tells me there's absolutely nothing to it – a *delightful* experience. He says that the moment he could he came to share the experience with us. It is like sunrise when you're camping out; the coming of color and illumination to widened spaces that were darkened. An enlarging and defining of the pattern of your own life. He could go on and on, but it's not the time to talk of it."

— 4 —

That is what newcomers to the land have had to say. In addition we had a considerable body of report from Betty, while she was still here with us, but venturing across as a tourist, so to speak. Experimental dying, the Invisibles called it. Most of that has been fully set down already. I shall not repeat here, but shall refer those enough interested to The Betty Book, Across the Unknown, and The Road I Know.

Still further, we had a certain amount of incidental comment by the old-timers in the invisible. The ideas of most importance to the present discussion seemed to be that (a) we cross over Just as we are now, (b) there is no sudden illumination of knowledge, (c) our status is determined by what sort of an "outfit for eternity" we have gathered for ourselves here on earth.

"The thing to emphasize," the Invisible told us, "is continuity here, not hereafter. No sudden jump will transform you. You take over what you are, which is the real continuity. It is not the continuity of going over to something easier and adapted to all your peculiarities. It is a smooth transition. You might just as well accept it. You've got to do away with the superstition that your handicaps here will be instantly eliminated there. Get adapted here and you will enter without conditions. You might just as well get to work here. It is a smooth beautiful thing, this continuity. The division between the lives is an imaginary line, like the equator."

And another time:

"Take a recognized experience, like dying.

Supposing it had come to you, and you stood the other side of bodily death. What a turmoil of readjustment in values there would be! You are there dependent on your bodily life for almost all your occupations and interests and the very content of your daily consciousness. Therefore, all those remain with your body when you leave it. Now, standing on the other side, what have you as the *result* of those daily occupations and interests? Many dim things; but undeveloped, and undirected. In face of the big unusual issues one feels very empty-handed and empty-hearted, hopelessly ineffectual.

"You remember the experimental dying, and how you set up housekeeping with the few things you had brought along of realities – volition, patience, perseverance, loving-kindness, whatever you had of enduring qualities – and by the exercise of them created your new environment? Well, you don't have to go so far imaginatively as that. You can imagine yourself, as happens to many, suddenly transplanted, an emigrant, a refugee, any example of a suddenly uprooted being hustled into a radically changed environment. Place yourself in imagination in Smyrna or Palestine or Timbuktu or any other part of the world – without luggage!

"Adjustment comes about in many ways. The action is entirely dependent on the mental and spiritual capital you have brought with you. Examples might help.

"Let us consider someone from the lower grades, for instance, who is without firmly established supporting convictions previously developed through having constructed his own firm conditions of maintenance anywhere; without the eternal verity of equilibrium; without the surrounding stability of confidence in his own power of summoning to himself the same replacement conditions anywhere. He will begin at once to disintegrate and throw into confusion his whole creative mechanism by tearing it up into little worry-bits as to food and every detail of present and future need and his lack of possession of them at the moment. His panic over his mechanism of reconstructing his life puts him at once into the conditions he fears.

"Then there is a certain type of oversane, overcautious, unintentioned people who have never sensed intangible verities, who prefer to occupy themselves exclusively with the more limited ponderables; just as there are the unfortunates who have never sensed the rapture of a perfume or the ecstasy of a color harmony or who are deaf to sound reactions. Let us accept them in friendly understanding. They are useful people in keeping ponderable stability. But they will have to begin slowly over here."

One of the advantages of our instruction with the Invisibles was supposed to be the elimination of much of the confusion of readjustment.

"You see," the Invisible explained this, "little by little, bit by bit, we are giving you life in its extension into the next phase, and how to go about creating your future conditions, just as you create them there for ordinary living. Do not be abashed by your own ponderable mind, any more than you are abashed by the ponderable people. Escape frequently from its limitations and capture a small boy's enjoyment in, constructing yourself a tree house, a habitation after your own heart above your ordinary dwelling place. Some day you may inhabit that ideal structure; but at any rate you will return to the misfit with fresh energy and strength for reconstructing it more in keeping with the ideal one.

"I did not touch on the positive side of the emigration to Smyrna, or Palestine or Timbuktu, how the developed person would go about it, because it is totally impossible to convince anybody who has not attained the creative power, that it will work."

As for death itself, as a phenomenon, the Invisibles actually seemed to be little interested. The one we call the Doctor once said that there is nothing to be wondered at in death, but that the fact of birth is indeed wonderful.

"Why can't you teach about it in a commonplace fashion?" complained another Invisible. "Why not say as to death that the life of each species is imprisoned in its fruit? Each fruit, the flesh, is the bearer of the seed. Why not think of your own seed of life within your flesh in the same way? The flesh is only the bearer of the seed to further development. It is healthy and normal to lie down to die as a seed plants itself. The healthier and stronger you get in spirit, the more beautiful all these things look to you."

"What," asked one of our visitors, "does death do to personality:"'

"It gives you greater and simpler opportunities for development," was the reply. "The mechanism, the apparatus you carry from your life for that purpose is that mechanism, and only that mechanism, that you have built by your constructive work. If you have not accomplished much constructive work, you approach those future opportunities crippled. But unlike earth cripples, you will have the ability, If you will use it, to heal yourself by appropriate effort. But the start you will make, and the breadth of opportunity you will enjoy will depend solely and entirely upon what you have done now."

"How about violent death, and its shock and pain?"

"The normal end of earth life is a ripening, by which the forces are withdrawn into the seed easily and naturally, to be divorced, in due time, from their rootings in the soil. But the strange interwoven pattern of existence does not always permit of this easy and graceful consummation. Many are cut off by accident and untoward chance before the sap of earth has ceased to flow. Such an accident, from the point of view of ordered progression, is to be regretted, but is in result little more than a check. The orientation of the entity is toward the forward trend of progression. The groping of his hands is toward the direction of progress; and so may be seized by those awaiting, and eased from the stumble into a resumption."

He made one exception to this comforting statement of aid: The Suicide.

"Those, however, who deliberately, and not by submission to accident beyond their control, take into their own hands the termination of prescribed experience are in a different class. The very renunciation of responsibilities exerts a magnetic attraction which reorients the psyche back toward those responsibilities. So that, in place of the impulse forward toward onward progress, the soul is bound, by an urge which it cannot overcome, to the backward view. Do not confuse this with the conventional picture of the 'earthbound' spirit. The longing of regret for opportunities now seen to have been thrown away – the opportunities for certain fulfillments – blinds the entity to the possibility of those same fulfillments, with greater labor and lesser opportunity to be sure, in another state of being. Until that fixation is resolved, the entity is static and impervious to the helpful influences that so quickly heal the victims of a purely accidental passing.

"To that extent, and to that extent only, is he cut off from those who would help him on this side. His help must come from that toward which his attention is thus drawn. Dilutedly, painfully, at second hand, he must make good his abandoned deficiencies, not from the abundance close about him, but from the meagerness he has deserted. This is not Justice'; it is the law."

But as to the normal process of dying, even in the case of violent death, even violent death with anticipation, as in a failing airplane, the Invisible was emphatic.

"There is *no* suffering," he insisted, "except possibly in the interim of falling. It is not always realized that, as far as this side is concerned, the shock of an untimely violent death furnishes its own anesthetic. *The process of death is never painful*, nor to be dreaded in any way. Don't worry about dying; you'll enjoy it!"

254

— 5 —

I shall close this chapter and this book with one more quotation from The Teller of Tales – a passage whose magic lends to all experience, of life or death, the mantle of Eternity.

"Vibrations are life, and waves am progress in life. The thing that is made by vibrations moves within the limits of its being, and also carries forward – through itself and its contacts – the wave.

"Waves lift and fall, as well as move forward. And the particles that comprise them are also elevated and depressed, as well as carrying through themselves the forward movement. The rise and fall is in itself rhythmic and harmonious. Without it no forward movement is possible. This is a universal law – applying to the mighty and on-sweeping tide of cosmic evolution, and alike to the little ripples in the tiny pools that make up individual affairs. The sea gull that exults upward on the shoulder of the rising wave, too often, instead of falling in glory of grandeur into the trough, plunges from its height, darkened with despair; because it has not the vision to see nor the perception to feel the mighty, slow-gathering force that will lift it again to another moment of high-tossing, sun-glinted height.

"This is a universal law.

"Know that. Understand that. Accept the recession into the quiet hollow, into the slow sucking trough, as part of the great rhythm – without which there would be stagnation. Learn to take it as the repose period, the gathering period, the period in which the mighty forces that lift the wave upward, are quietly, powerfully coming in. If you could only once feel this, visualize it, never again could you be uneasy, depressed, low-spirited, discouraged, merely because of the natural, inevitable, necessary ebb after the flow. Never again would you worry because in this or that your powers of today are not your powers of yesterday, that your wings are folded, that a darkness seems to have closed you about. Accept the quietude, accept the ebb; enjoy it, as all harmonious things should be enjoyed. Rest in confidence, with your folded wings, knowing that it is the Law; that soon beneath your breast the stir of gathering forces must be felt. Sure that in the progress that the law ordains you must once more be swept upward to the glittering crest, whence all horizons are far, and the whistling winds of eternity tempt again your outspread wings.

"As I said, this is a universal law. By it you can measure your smallest moods. By it you can measure your greatest griefs and despairs. Carry it always with you. For its fitting is to all occasion."

The Unobstructed Universe

Stewart Edward White

Oxford City Press, 2010
Hardback, ISBN: 978-1-84902-650-5
Paperback, ISBN: 978-1-84902-766-3